DRIVING SURVIVAL

with
Jim MacPherson

AAA PUBLISHING

President & CEO	**Robert Darbelnet**
Executive Vice President,	**Rick Rinner**
Publishing & Administration	
Managing Director, Travel Information	**Bob Hopkins**

Director, Product Development	**Bill Wood**
Director, Sales	**John Coerper**
Director, Publishing Operations	**Susan Sears**
Director, Publishing Marketing	**Patty Wight**
Director, Purchasing & Corporate Services	**Becky Barrett**
Director, Tourism Information Development	**Michael Petrone**
Director, Travel Information	**Jeff Zimmerman**
Director, GIS/Cartography	**Jan Coyne**
Director, Development & Systems	**Ramin Kalhor**
Director, Business Development	**Gary Sisco**

Product Manager	**Lisa Spence**
Managing Editor	**Margaret Cavanaugh**

Manager, Sales & Market Development	**Bart Peluso**
AAA Travel Store & E-Store Manager	**Sharon Edwards**
Manager, Business Line Publicity	**Janie Graziani**
Print Buyer	**Laura Cox**
Manager, Product Support	**Linda Indolfi**

Project Editor	**Tracy Larson**
Illustrator and Graphic Designer	**Keri Caffrey**
Copy Editor	**G.K. Sharman**

Thanks to AAA Government Relations and Traffic Safety,
AAA Automotive and AAA Travel
and the Lake Mary, Fla., Police Department.

Copyright © 2003 AAA Publishing. All rights reserved.

ISBN 1-56251-752-X Stock Number 203303

Published by AAA Publishing, 1000 AAA Drive
Heathrow, Florida 32746

Printed in the USA by Quebecor World Inc.

About the Author

Jim MacPherson

Jim MacPherson writes more than 100 automotive columns each year for the readers of *The Hartford Courant*. Since 1987, he also has helped thousands of listeners of his radio program with advice on buying, servicing and repairing vehicles. For several years, he managed financial services for AAA Hartford/Cincinnati, where he was responsible for making thousands of loans for new and used vehicles. Jim also managed the AAA club's driver education and traffic safety programs. He is a licensed master driving instructor.

Other Books with Jim MacPherson

AAA Auto Guide: Buying or Leasing a Car

About the Illustrator

Keri Caffrey

Keri Caffrey operates her own professional design studio with a national client base. She has illustrated and designed boating safety publications for the U.S. Coast Guard as well as technical publications for clients in the aviation industry. Keri also works with hospitals, healthcare companies and community service organizations in designing and creating newsletters, advertisements, brochures, annual reports and on-screen presentations.

Table of Contents

Illustrations and Photographs

Introduction

Introduction

You Don't Need This Book, Right?

Millions of drivers like you crash their vehicles every year.

These collisions killed nearly 42,000 people and injured another 3 million people, according to the most recent figures available. A decade ago, more than 44,000 people died and another 5.4 million were injured on the nation's roads.

Although the statistics indicate traffic safety is improving significantly, don't let down your guard.

Perhaps the most disturbing fact to come out of recent statistics is that most people involved in fatal crashes are "good" drivers: Only 15 percent were in a previous accident, while nearly 59 percent had no previous convictions for motor vehicle offenses, according to a National Highway Traffic Safety Administration report.

In other words, they probably were a lot like you. Their good records didn't prevent them from crashing, yet most of the accidents were caused by driver error.

The principle of *driving survival* recognizes that most crashes result from errors made by "good" drivers who often have years of experience behind the wheel. Maybe they picked up bad habits or forgot important fundamentals, and there's a good chance they — and probably you, too — were trained improperly for contemporary vehicles, traffic patterns, driving environments and laws.

To survive in today's traffic, you must overcome these deficiencies.

Driving survival means embracing new habits and approaches to driving — and thereby reducing your likelihood of dying or being injured.

The costs associated with crashing, measured in both physical pain and dollars lost, are staggering. Accident victims' medical bills paid under employer-provided health insurance have reached $32.6 billion, according to the National Highway Traffic Safety Administration's economic study of motor-vehicle crashes. Need more reasons to adopt a driving survival mindset?

- The American Society of Safety Engineers cites traffic crashes as the largest single cause of on-the-job deaths.

- Traffic accidents are the leading cause of death for 1- to 34-year-olds, according to data from the Centers for Disease Control and Prevention.

- According to a University of Oklahoma police study, you are more likely to be involved in an accident than to be a crime victim.

- The total bill for all crashes is estimated to top $230 billion a year.

Getting Set Behind the Wheel

In This Chapter

• • • • • • • • • • •

- How to adjust the seat and mirrors for maximum safety

- Why you shouldn't think of the device on top of your seat back as a "head rest"

- How to cope with a vehicle that doesn't fit you comfortably

- How to minimize the effects of blind spots

For a driver, one vehicle is pretty much like another, right? One size fits all. Not necessarily. While not as personal as a pair of shoes, a vehicle still has to "fit" the driver. How many crashes are caused by drivers who don't have a good fit behind the wheel? No one knows.

We do know, however, that proper adjustment of the seat, mirrors and seat belts is critical to your safety, comfort and enjoyment. It gives you a good view of the road ahead and behind, as well as the lanes to either side. It lets you reach all the controls easily without having to take your eyes and attention from the road. It means you can be comfortable, even on longer drives, and that the seat belts provide optimal protection.

With a good fit, your seat effectively communicates what the car is doing as you start, stop and turn. And if the unthinkable happens and you are involved in a crash, it means the safety systems will give you the most protection possible.

Adjust Your Seat

Move the seat back and forth until you find a position that lets you reach the pedals easily. If you can operate the accelerator and brake without lifting your heel from the floor, you've got it right.

You should be able to reach the floor beneath the brake pedal with your right foot. This means you'll be able to pump the brake over its full range of motion in an emergency.

> **SAFETY** While much of this chapter deals with adjustments you should make inside your car, your job as a driver starts as you approach your vehicle. Look for obvious problems, such as a low tire, broken light or puddle of oil or coolant. If you spot any potential problem, have it checked before you drive.

In some vehicles, you also can adjust the height of the seat. Sit high enough to have a good view of the road ahead of and behind your vehicle. Your shoulders should be at the same height or slightly higher than the top of the steering wheel.

If you're tall, lower the seat so the inside rearview mirror doesn't block a portion of your view through the windshield. If you're short, raise it enough so that the driver's side mirror doesn't block your view of traffic coming from the left.

In some vehicles, you can push a button or two to adjust the seat height automatically. In others, you'll have to manipulate levers and cranks manually from inside or outside the vehicle. Sometimes you may have to call on a repair technician to do it for you.

Next, adjust the angle of the backrest. Sit as upright as is comfortable, but don't sit too close to the steering wheel.

How do you know if you've got it right? Hold your arms straight out with your elbows locked and your shoulders not thrown forward. If you can touch the top of the wheel with your wrists, you're in the right position. If you can't, see if you can adjust the height of the steering wheel or the angle of the seat back. Some steering wheels will also telescope to help you get a better fit.

DID YOU KNOW? Much of the public's attention has focused on the proper distance between a driver and the air bag in the hub of the steering wheel. However, sitting too close to a non-air-bag-equipped steering wheel carries its own risks. In a severe crash, your body will move forward, even if you are properly belted in. Sitting too close to the steering wheel increases the odds that you will strike it, perhaps too quickly and too hard to escape injury.

If your vehicle has an air bag in the steering wheel, you should sit 10 to 12 inches from the hub of the wheel, according to most vehicle manufacturers' guidelines. Check the owner's manual for your model's specific recommendations. Also, line up the steering wheel so that the air bag would deploy toward your chest. This generally means lowering the steering wheel. After you adjust the seat and steering wheel, use a tape measure to determine the distance between your sternum and the hub of the wheel.

> **SAFETY** Although they can save lives, air bags also can be dangerous if you or your passengers fail to appreciate their power. Leaning forward to get a better view of traffic at intersections puts you too close to the air bag — a bad idea if it deploys. Instead, drive forward 8 to 12 more inches. Rarely will this maneuver put you at risk of cross traffic. Additionally, passengers who rest their feet on the dash or lean against a door panel or seat bolster containing a side air bag also put themselves at risk of harm. Never place a child in a front seat with a passenger-side air bag.

The federal government allows motorists to disconnect the air bag if they can't sit far enough from it, but doing this may not be your best choice.

Your last adjustment is the head restraint position. What most people call a "head rest" is part of a modern vehicle's safety system. It's designed to minimize injuries in some types of collisions, but works only if you adjust it correctly.

Ideally, the top of the head restraint should be even with the top of your head. At the very least, the top of the restraint should be higher than the center of your head or just above your ears. In addition, make sure that it's no more than 3.5 inches from the back of your head. Positioned lower or farther back, it can't offer you full protection.

Getting Set Behind the Wheel

The seat is adjusted to enable the driver to easily reach the pedals and to position his chest 10 to 12 inches from the hub of the steering wheel. The head restraint is even with the top of his head, and his seat belt is fastened snugly across his hips.

In some cars, head restraints are fixed. In others, they can be adjusted but won't lock when raised or moved forward, which means they likely will collapse when you need them most — in a rear-end collision. Manufacturers are starting to outfit some vehicles with "active head-restraint systems," in which the restraint travels forward with the seat occupant in a crash and "catches" the head as it snaps backward.

Fasten Your Seat Belt

A good seat-belt fit is about more than just comfort. It's also a matter of safety.

The National Highway Traffic Safety Administration estimates that 11,900 Americans involved in accidents survive each year because they wear seat belts. In cars, properly used lap and shoulder belts can reduce a front passenger's risk of fatal injury by 45 percent and can reduce the risk of moderate to critical injury by 50 percent, according to U.S. Department of Transportation research. In trucks, the reduction in risk is even greater. Seat belts help prevent passengers from being ejected in a crash, a tragic consequence that kills three-quarters of those to whom it happens. They also keep the driver behind the wheel so a deploying air bag can serve its purpose.

Wear the lap portion low across your hips — never across your stomach. The shoulder belt should cross your shoulder, not your neck. Increasingly, new cars and trucks come equipped with height-adjustable shoulder belts, at least for the driver and front-seat passenger. These belts make it easier for many people to get a good fit. Never wear the shoulder portion under your arm or behind your back, and never use a harness clip or other device designed to prevent neck or shoulder irritation or wrinkled clothes by locking slack into the shoulder portion of the belt.

Adjusting Your Seat Belt

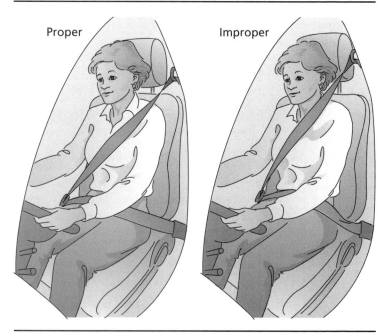

Proper   Improper

The proper use of a seat belt requires the lap portion of the seat belt fit low and snug across the hips, never across the stomach, and the shoulder belt should cross the shoulder rather than the neck.

In the back seat, occupants who buckle up not only reduce their own risk of injury, they also reduce front-seat occupants' risk of death by five times.

Buckle up Children

Motor-vehicle crashes are the No. 1 killer of American children. According to the most recent data, more than 2,300 children ages 14 and younger died and nearly

300,000 were injured in crashes — an average of six children killed and nearly 800 hurt each day.

The death and injury figures could be cut in half each year if every child passenger were properly restrained, according to National Transportation Safety Board estimates.

AAA recommends that as children mature physically, they progress through four stages of occupant protection. These stages depend on a child's age, weight and height and are in keeping with AAA policy and the best practices of safety experts, including the National Highway Traffic Safety Administration and the American Academy of Pediatrics. Always buckle children in the back seat, the safest position in a vehicle, and never install a child-safety seat in a pickup truck's insufficiently stable "jump seat."

Rear-Facing Child Safety Seat

Always restrain children up to age 1 *and* who weigh up to 20 pounds in a federally approved, properly installed, rear-facing child-safety seat. It's a good idea to use the rear-facing seat as long as possible. While developmental progress makes age the more important factor, a child must meet both age and weight requirements before progressing to a forward-facing seat.

The rear-facing position supports a child's head, neck and back and reduces neck and spinal cord stress in a crash. Never place a rear-facing seat in front of an air bag.

If no other seating option is available, disconnect the air bag and push the seat back as far as possible.

Forward-Facing Child Safety Seat

Children over age 1 and weighing more than 20 pounds should be restrained in a federally approved, properly installed, forward-facing child-safety seat until they reach 40 pounds — usually about age 4. Internal harness systems in these seats keep a child properly restrained, and snug straps limit the child's forward motion. In a crash, the forward-facing position evenly distributes physical forces over a child's body.

Booster Seat

Safety experts call for children between ages 4 and 8 who weigh more than 40 pounds and who are shorter than 4 feet 9 inches to be restrained in a booster seat. Research shows that poorly fitting adult seat belts can injure children. Booster seats minimize the risk by helping to ensure proper seat belt placement.

The federal government is studying booster seats to determine whether they're also good protection for children who weigh more than 50 pounds. Although booster seats are adequate for smaller children, their effectiveness for kids over 50 pounds is unclear. AAA supports additional research.

Lap and Shoulder Belt

Properly restrain children younger than age 13 in the back seat. Studies show that buckling up in the back decreases a child's risk of being killed in a crash by one-third. Never place a child in front of an air bag. Teenagers should wear lap and shoulder belts, no matter where they sit.

Adjust the Mirrors

If your rearview mirror reflects everything you could see if you were looking out the back window, it's adjusted correctly. If you think the view in your side mirrors should duplicate much of what you can see from the inside mirror, you're like a lot of your fellow motorists — but unfortunately, you're wrong.

Adjusting the Side Mirrors

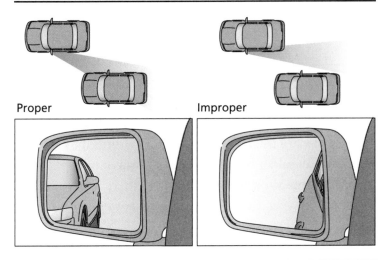

Proper   Improper

In a properly adjusted side mirror, your vehicle's fender shouldn't be visible. Instead, you should see an expanded view to the side of your vehicle that reduces blind spots.

Side mirrors should expand your view to the side of your vehicle and reduce blind spots. If you can see your fenders in the side mirrors, the mirrors are misadjusted.

For a better side view, try this technique. To adjust the left outside mirror, lean to the left so your head almost touches the driver's door window. Adjust the mirror so you can barely see your car's left rear fender. When you return to your normal seating position, you shouldn't see any part of your vehicle in that mirror. To adjust the right outside mirror, lean 4 to 8 inches to the right and adjust the mirror so you can barely see the right rear fender. Again, when you return to your normal position, you should see none of the right side of your vehicle.

Reduce Blind Spots

Blind spots are defined as any space outside your car that you can't see. They can be caused by your car's structure or limits in your peripheral vision. Although properly adjusted mirrors can reduce blind spots, they can't eliminate them. That's why you still need to glance over your shoulder before changing lanes or merging. This is especially true on multi-lane roads where a driver two or more lanes away could be planning to merge into the spot you want to occupy.

These head checks should be done by glancing quickly over your shoulder in the direction you want go. Look only long enough to verify that there is no vehicle there and nothing moving in from another lane.

Blind Spots

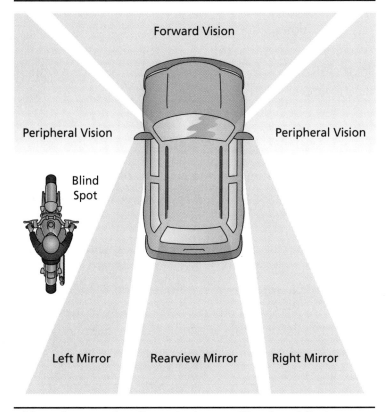

Although properly adjusted mirrors will reduce blind spots, they can't eliminate them. In this overhead view, the motorcyclist is in the driver's blind spot.

Some vehicles have larger blind spots than others. Thick pillars or panels on either side of your windshield can hide a pedestrian who is close to you or a car that is farther away. The closer the left pillar is to your eyes, the more it can hide.

Large pillars between the side windows in the back and the rear window can hide an approaching car as you back out of a parking space. This is a major problem in some convertibles when the top is up and in many vans and sport-utility vehicles. These panels also can hide a vehicle during lane changes and merges.

Fix Problems in an Ill-Fitting Vehicle

Proper positioning lets you comfortably place your hands on the lower half of the steering wheel with your elbows close to your side at a comfortable, natural bend.

If, after making all the necessary adjustments, you find that your vehicle doesn't fit your body, you're not alone. Some vehicle owners may not understand what constitutes a good fit; others may not know that a different make or model would have been a far better choice.

PITFALLS When a 6-foot, 7-inch man complained that no car offered sufficient head room, I gave him a list of models that might accommodate his height. Off he went to take a look. Two weeks later he had more complaints. While he fit in most vehicles on the list, he was still unhappy. "I wouldn't be seen in any of them," he said. One was a minivan, another a compact more popular with women than men, and so on. His questionable solution was to put form over function — or in this case, fashion over safety — and buy a trendy but ill-fitting sport-utility vehicle with a roof liner that constantly rubbed his head.

In most cases, the people with such a problem are shorter, taller or heavier than average. However, some "average-size" people have a problem, too. It makes sense to shop for a car or truck that fits.

If you own a car that doesn't fit you well, it's possible to address specific problems.

Have the Seat Remounted

If you can't raise the driver's seat so your shoulders are about the same height as the top of the steering wheel, check to see if the seat can be remounted in a higher position. Few vehicles allow this, and a repair technician probably will have to do the work for you. If raising the seat isn't possible, find a firm, wedge-shaped cushion to sit on. Many department and auto-parts stores sell cushions designed specifically for this purpose. Remember: A cushion that is too soft may cause comfort problems during daily use and cause safety problems in a crash.

Overcome Mirror Problems

If the inside mirror blocks your view of traffic approaching from the right — often a problem for tall drivers who own lower, sporty models — adjust it, if possible, at both the mirror and windshield ends of the short shaft that holds the mirror to the glass. Doing so lets you push the mirror up, out of the way of your forward view of traffic. If the shaft is fixed at the windshield mounting point, you may be able to rotate a non-electronic mirror 180 degrees so it is upside down. This often will raise the mirror enough to reduce, if not eliminate, the problem. The day-night lever then will be on the top of the mirror.

You probably won't be able to rotate an electronic mirror — one that dims automatically at night, displays the outside temperature, shows your direction or contains reading lights. To compensate, be especially careful at intersections and when driving through parking lots. You'll have to duck and look under the mirror to get a complete view of what's in front of the vehicle.

Short Drivers

COURTESY OF INSURANCE INSTITUTE FOR HIGHWAY SAFETY

Rather than deactivate the driver's side air bag, short drivers should push the seat back as far as possible to lengthen the distance between their chest and the hub of the steering wheel to at least 10 inches. If this is insufficient, adjust the pedals, if possible, or install pedal extenders.

Extend the Pedals

If you can't sit at least 10 inches from the air bag, try extending the pedals. Some newer car models have adjustable pedals, but in most cases, you'll have to bolt inexpensive extenders to the accelerator, brake and clutch.

In some cars, the seat will sink lower as you move it back, so you also may need to add a cushion.

Use a Seat Cushion

If the outside driver's mirror is permanently fixed and blocks your view of traffic coming from the left, your best bet may be a seat cushion that boosts you enough to see over it. Drivers who experience this problem frequently find that their shoulders are below the top of the steering wheel as well.

Adjust the Back of the Seat

If you lack adequate head room, ask the car dealer whether a seat mounting option would lower the cushion. If not, adjusting the seat back sometimes works. Don't recline too far, as this will compromise your ability to control the vehicle and also could affect the protection offered by seat belts and air bags in a crash.

Install More Mirrors

If the mirrors have inadequate range, install additional mirrors. A convex (fisheye) mirror should be used only to assist with parking and low-speed maneuvers. If attached on top of your mirror, it will reduce that mirror's usefulness.

If physical limitations make it painful for you to look over your shoulder before changing lanes, additional mirrors can help. Some states may require such mirrors to be installed on any vehicle you own, and that the restriction be listed on your license as a condition of driving.

Extend the Seat Belt

If the seat belt is too short, ask the manufacturer about an extender or have a qualified technician permanently install a seat belt with more webbing. If, while shopping for a new car or truck, you find a vehicle that fits you in all ways except for the seat belt length, check to see if either of these options is available.

Chapter 2

Managing Risk While Driving

In This Chapter

• • • • • • • • • • • •

- Why you should become a "risk manager"

- What common situations hide potential hazards

- Tips for nighttime driving

For years, you've been told to drive defensively — to anticipate other drivers' sometimes foolish actions and respond to them. But a defensive strategy isn't the only tactic you must use. Understand that you are always at risk.

Don't become complacent and forget that risk is always present when you drive. Your perception of what's dangerous isn't always accurate. Driving is a social event. Because you constantly interact with other drivers, you share your risk with everyone else.

You can increase or decrease your level of risk. In effect, you must become a risk manager while driving.

Learn to Manage Your Risk While Driving

Fifty years ago, Harold L. Smith, road safety instructor for the Ford Motor Co., urged drivers to adopt a routine of looking at the road immediately in front, scanning far ahead and then checking either the conditions at the side of the road, traffic to the rear or the instruments before repeating the sequence again and again. The "Smith System" also called for drivers to adjust steering based on the view of the road far ahead, to maintain an escape path and to signal so other motorists would know what to expect.

> **DID YOU KNOW?**
>
> Many driving manuals require students to remember IPDE, which stands for **I**dentify potential hazards, **P**redict how other drivers' actions or road changes might affect you, **D**ecide how to avoid potential problems and **E**xecute an action plan that keeps the situation from becoming dangerous. More recently, some manuals have added "S" for **S**can the road. However, scanning isn't enough for effective risk managers. You must search the road ahead to identify potential hazards.

Search Far Ahead

To anticipate potential problems — traffic that has come to an unexpected standstill, for instance — search for them well in advance. Scan at least 20 to 30 seconds down the road. In town at lower speeds, that corresponds to about one or two blocks. On the highway at higher speeds, it means about a half-mile.

Know What's in Front of You

Become completely aware of everything 12 to 15 seconds ahead of you. Think of this zone as your immediate operating arena. This would translate to about a block ahead when you're driving in town or a quarter-mile on the highway.

Look to the Sides in Front of You

As you search ahead, concentrate not only on the pavement but also on the sides of the road. People, animals and vehicles could suddenly occupy your lane.

Note vehicles that may be entering the road or slowing to leave it, as well as pedestrians, animals, bicyclists and objects that could block your view of potential hazards. Also take note of changes in the width or character of the highway and its shoulders.

Search to the Rear

Not all troubles are ahead of you. Knowing what is behind you is important, too. Remember, between one-quarter and one-third of all two-vehicle crashes are rear-end collisions.

Leave Space Ahead

Searching far enough ahead, to the sides and rear will alert you to most potential problems. However, if you don't leave enough space around your vehicle to react properly once you see a problem, you aren't effectively managing your risk. How much space is enough? AAA recommends that you leave at least a three-second gap between your vehicle and the car in front. During rush hour on many highways, it is not unusual to see motorists leave just a half-second or less between their front bumper and the vehicle ahead — not nearly enough to be safe.

To determine the distance in seconds between your car and the car in front, count it out. When the car ahead passes a landmark — for instance, a strip in the road or a light pole — count "one thousand one, one thousand two, one thousand three." If your car reaches the landmark before you finish saying "...one thousand three," you're following too closely. Similarly, when you scan 30 seconds

Visual Control Zone

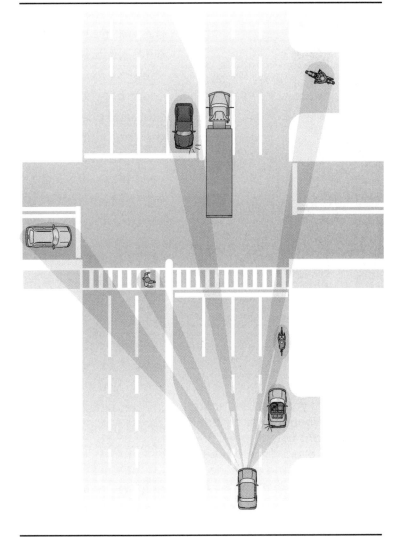

Particularly on urban, suburban and rural highways, you will
need to devise simultaneous plans for dealing with
numerous potentially dangerous situations, such as the
vehicle to the right changing lanes to avoid the bicyclist, the
pedestrian continuing through the crosswalk, or the
oncoming driver making a left turn.

Three-Second Gap

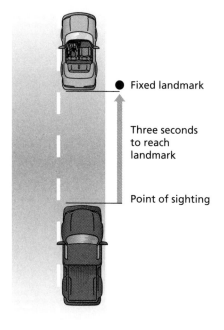

Fixed landmark

Three seconds
to reach
landmark

Point of sighting

If a problem arises, a three-second gap between your vehicle and the one in front should give you time and space to react. When the car ahead passes a light pole or other landmark, count "one thousand one, one thousand two, one thousand three." You shouldn't reach the landmark before you finish counting.

down the road, note an object by the side of the road that is at the outer reaches of your scanning zone. Then count from "one thousand one" to "one thousand thirty." If you reach the object before you finish counting, expand your view of the road ahead.

Leave Space to One Side

By leaving space to at least one side, in addition to the three-second gap outlined above, you give yourself a second means of escape in an emergency. It also means you will be able to move to one side to defuse a potential problem before it develops.

In many ways, managing risk is a state of mind. You have to be alert, aware of your surroundings and constantly engaged in a two-step process of looking for potential problems and developing ways to handle looming difficulties. The best approach is to eliminate a problem before it develops. However, you also should have a backup plan in case another motorist, pedestrian or animal does something unexpected.

Be Alert at Intersections

There's no shortage of ways to practice your risk-management skills.

As you approach an intersection where you have the right of way, recognize that a stop sign or a red light can't physically stop an oncoming car. The driver must see the sign or signal, apply the brake pedal, have a car with operating brakes and be driving on a road with sufficient traction to bring the car to a halt.

Just one missing element in this series could cause that oncoming vehicle to crash into your car. In the most recent year documented, federal statistics showed that 2.7 million crashes occurred at intersections, resulting in 8,400 deaths and 995,000 injuries. In other words, more than five crashes happened every minute of every day at intersections.

Common sense demands that you actively search for motorists who are about to run a stop sign or signal when you pass through an intersection. Also, don't trust that a

Dangerous Intersection

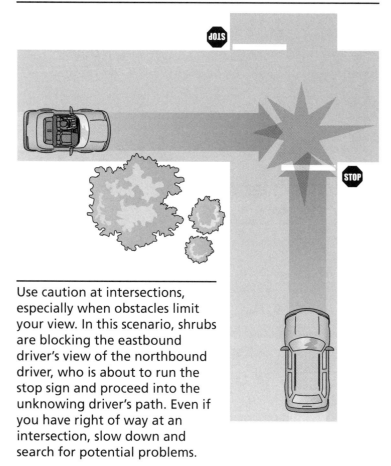

Use caution at intersections, especially when obstacles limit your view. In this scenario, shrubs are blocking the eastbound driver's view of the northbound driver, who is about to run the stop sign and proceed into the unknowing driver's path. Even if you have right of way at an intersection, slow down and search for potential problems.

blinking turn signal means a driver will turn. The signal may have been left on inadvertently, or the driver could suddenly change course without canceling the signal.

In many cases, being prepared means slowing down until you can confirm that an oncoming car will stop. Remove your foot from the accelerator and position it over the brake so you can stop quickly, if need be. Placing your foot over the brake can reduce your reaction time by as much as a full second, which would reduce your total stopping distance 44 feet if you were traveling at 30 mph. That could be the difference between life and death.

In other cases, being prepared might mean swerving to avoid a vehicle coming through the red light. Is the lane for oncoming traffic clear and therefore open to you? Is there space to the right — another lane, a shoulder or a suburban lawn? These alternatives all are fair game if they enable you to avoid a potentially deadly crash. What's not an option is a route closed by another vehicle, a pedestrian or a bicyclist.

Compensate for Restricted Vision

Restricted vision is another challenge.

Blind spots can result from your vehicle's structure, such as pillars beside the windshield. Trees, shrubs, buildings and parked vehicles can limit your field of view. Lighting can cause problems: Turn into the sun or face an oncoming motorist who fails to dim his high beams and you can be temporarily blinded.

Obstructions also can restrict vision. I have evaluated a frightening number of licensed drivers who don't understand that a vehicle may be speeding toward them even though they can't see it.

During one behind-the-wheel evaluation, I took a driver who had been involved in several crashes to an intersection where a bridge abutment made it difficult to see traffic coming from the left. The woman stopped properly, looked to the left, the right and then left again. When she didn't notice any oncoming vehicles, she started through the intersection. I stopped the car with the instructor's brake, told her to move the car forward a few more feet and had her do a more thorough search for oncoming traffic. She then saw a line of cars whose drivers would have had to take evasive action had she entered the intersection.

At the same time, of course, the other drivers were speeding down the highway, trusting that no one would venture into their path from behind the abutment. None of the drivers involved was being a good risk manager.

Vehicles waiting in the middle of an intersection to turn often can block your view of oncoming traffic and make it impossible for other drivers to see you. Neither you nor an oncoming driver can afford to assume that the vehicle waiting to turn isn't hiding another car or truck. Never take for granted that the coast is clear — always confirm that nothing is coming.

Be particularly careful in areas where a dip in the road just before an intersection could hide a vehicle. Even if the dip is too shallow to completely mask a car or truck, it still could obscure your view of a motorcyclist.

Adapt Quickly if Road Narrows

The width of your travel lane can change for many reasons. Construction, potholes, parked vehicles, a motorist who drives or stops outside his lane and the design of the road itself can take away space you thought was available for your car. Managing risk requires you to anticipate these possibilities and then take appropriate action.

Cars parked by the side of the road can reduce maneuvering space. Add an approaching vehicle that seems on track to meet you just as you reach the parked car, and you will need to act immediately.

Changing your speed usually does the trick. By slowing, you let the oncoming vehicle pass the parked car before you get to it. Speeding up gets you past the width reduction before you meet the other car. If you become sandwiched between the parked car and an oncoming vehicle, you won't be able to steer away if the oncoming car drifts toward you or the parked car's driver suddenly decides to enter traffic.

There are times, of course, when you face a line of oncoming vehicles rather than just one. If you have enough space to pass between the oncoming traffic and the parked car, slow down and move your vehicle farther from the side that would present more serious consequences in a crash — generally this means moving farther from the oncoming traffic. If the danger is equal on both sides, center your car in the available space. If you don't have enough space to move safely between, stop and wait for all the oncoming vehicles to pass before continuing.

Keep Escape Routes Open

Maintain at least two escape routes when possible. You can always change speed — accelerating, slowing or stopping. In addition, make sure you can steer to at least one alternative route in an emergency.

Here is an example of how to analyze potential escape routes. An oncoming car is nearing as you drive down a suburban street. In all likelihood, nothing unusual will happen. However, as soon as you spot the car, you start considering options. First, quickly estimate the exact spot where your vehicles will pass. If the other driver were to enter your lane at the last second, would you be able to steer to the right at that spot? If not, gradually speed up or slow down so you have space to steer.

Why wouldn't you be able to steer away? Trees, a pedestrian, a deep gully, a parked vehicle or any of countless other obstructions could box you in. Incidentally, steering left into the oncoming traffic lane isn't advisable. When the other driver realizes he's in your lane, his first move will be to return to his lane as quickly as possible.

Escape routes are often anything but inviting. Although an evasive maneuver into an open field may give you a rough ride and damage your car, the alternative — crashing into another vehicle — is likely to mean an even rougher ride, more vehicle damage and a higher probability of injuries.

Sometimes no clear escape path exists. Instead, several unattractive options confront you. Always opt for what would inflict the least damage.

Here are some suggestions:

• Steer toward something soft, light or flimsy, rather than something hard or heavy. Shrubs are a better option than a big tree trunk. Trash cans or a newspaper vending machine are more forgiving than a telephone pole.

• Steer toward something that can be moved rather than something stationary. If you're forced to choose between an unoccupied parked car or a large tree, aim for the car. Metal will bend and the vehicle will move forward with the force of the impact, reducing the stresses to your body.

SAFETY In emergencies, focus on where you want to go, not what you want to avoid hitting. People tend to steer in the direction they look. Concentrating on the stately oak tree you want to avoid only increases the likelihood that you'll hit it. Instead, focus on the path around the tree.

- Steer toward something stationary rather than something coming at you. Given the options of an unoccupied parked car or an oncoming vehicle, choose the parked car.

- If you must hit another vehicle, steer toward one going in your direction rather than one coming toward you.

- If you must hit an immovable object or an oncoming vehicle, a glancing blow or sideswipe is almost always preferable to a head-on collision. Striking another vehicle in front of the front axle or behind the rear axle increases the likelihood that the vehicle will spin, which will dissipate the impact's energy.

- If you must leave the road, stay in control. Don't lock your brakes and skid off the road. To accomplish this in a car without antilock brakes, lift your foot from the brake pedal just as you leave the pavement so you can steer. Non-paved surfaces, such as grass and dirt, give you far less traction than an asphalt or concrete road. By releasing your brakes as you leave the pavement, you make it easier to control the direction your car takes and steer around potentially deadly obstructions, such as trees. Once you have set your course, return to braking.

Use the Mirrors

Proper use of the mirrors is critical to risk management while driving. If cars that pass you from the rear or that seem to suddenly appear in your mirrors often surprise you, you aren't checking the mirrors enough. Be aware of every vehicle coming up from the rear before it gets near your car. Scan your mirrors every two to five seconds in traffic. In addition, check your mirrors frequently when descending a hill, when you slow or brake and before any lane change or other change in your direction or position on the road.

Also look behind you for big trucks. In an emergency, big trucks take twice as long to stop as passenger cars do. It boils down to basic physics, but many drivers don't grasp the concept that stopping a truck, which has much more mass than a car, requires a much greater distance.

If the truck gets too close, let the driver pass you. If that isn't possible, leave an even larger gap between your car and the vehicle in front of you so you can take longer to stop in an emergency. The tailgating 18-wheeler at your rear will need every extra inch you can give it.

Also recognize that a big truck on your back bumper closes one of your potential escape routes. You can't slam on the brakes to stop quickly.

Know Your Limitations at Night

Driving at night challenges all drivers. Darkness limits visibility, fatigue is a constant companion and night is when many people drink before getting behind the wheel. As a result, night driving is three times as dangerous as daylight driving. Although the number of vehicles on the road drops significantly between 6 p.m. and 6 a.m., nearly half of all crash fatalities occur during these hours.

Your view of what's ahead will be limited by how much pavement your headlights illuminate. Equally important, you must overcome the blinding glare of oncoming headlights. Because they have trouble seeing in dim light or recovering quickly after exposure to glare, some drivers who see adequately in the daytime may find nighttime driving difficult. Many states give drivers with nighttime vision problems a restricted license that's valid only for daytime use. To see well at night, a 50-year-old may need twice the light that a 30-year-old does.

Dirt can block up to 90 percent of the light that headlights emit and seriously limit your nighttime visibility. Clean your headlights whenever you clean your windshield.

Headlights do a mediocre job of illuminating the road immediately ahead of you and are almost worthless for seeing well to the sides of your vehicle. Roadside problems such as a dark-clothed pedestrian or a deer may not show up until the last second. You also may have trouble finding driveways and intersecting streets. Even sharp corners on unlighted roads can present problems.

The only way to cope with this reduced vision is to slow down. Far too many motorists overdrive their headlights — that is, they drive so fast that they can't stop or take evasive action when the headlights reveal an obstacle, such as an opossum crossing the road. Don't be one of these drivers. If you can't see at least four seconds ahead, reduce your speed.

SAFETY
While a three-second following distance is adequate during the day, at night you should double the gap between your car and the vehicle ahead. A six-second margin gives you a wider range of evasive opportunities in an emergency. It also gives you more time to recognize possible problems, which are harder to see in the dark.

When you scan ahead at night, look into the darkness beyond the light your headlights provide. You might see movement in the shadows.

In some situations, you also can use the tail lights of a car far in front to gauge what's ahead. If something, perhaps a pedestrian or another vehicle beyond your headlights' range, ventures onto the road between you and the car in front of you, it will block your view of the other vehicle's tail lights, at least temporarily. This sudden disappearance of tail lights should warn you that something is happening ahead. You also can use the reflections of oncoming cars' headlights in some road surfaces for the same purpose.

When facing an oncoming driver who doesn't dim high beams, keep looking ahead but shift your gaze to the right shoulder to avoid being blinded by the glare. Don't retaliate by refusing to dim your headlights. That will ensure only that two blinded drivers pass in the night.

In some cases, the driver who is blinding you may be using low beams. A heavy load in the trunk or poorly aimed headlights could be the problem.

Driving at night is easier when your windows, mirrors and headlight lenses are clean. First remove dirt, grease, oil and dust from the outside of the glass, then attack the stubborn film that forms on the inside of car windows. Cleaning just one side of the glass is of little use.

Accept that you can't safely overcome fatigue. You are most likely to tire when you normally eat dinner and at your usual bedtime. The later it gets, the more likely fatigue will impair you. According to recent statistics, fatal crashes involved 1,773 drivers judged to be tired or asleep or thought to have lost consciousness.

Avoid Distractions

Smart drivers don't operate a vehicle while distracted. They keep their mind and eyes on the road at all times.

Nearly every driver has made mistakes that can be blamed on distractions. Missing a turn, running off the road and reacting too slowly to a driver stopped in front of you all can happen when your attention is somewhere other than on the road.

SAFETY

In addition to facing often-debilitating fatigue at dinner and bedtime, most people also become tired in the afternoon, a body's normal down time. Attribute it to your circadian rhythm, which is linked to Earth's rotation. Plan trips so that you aren't on the road when you're normally sluggish. If you suffer from a sleep disorder, talk to your physician before you drive. Remember: You can't control your sleep cycles. Nodding off while driving or entering a fatigue-induced trance can be fatal.

How serious is this issue?

- Distracted drivers factor in 25 percent to 50 percent of all vehicle crashes, which means at least 1.5 million of the 6.5 million crashes reported each year are related to distracted drivers, according to the National Highway Traffic Safety Administration.

- NHTSA has found that the social and economic costs for these crashes are approaching an estimated $40 billion annually.

- An average person spends an hour and 13 minutes each day behind the wheel of an automobile, according to a report by the U.S. Department of Transportation Federal Highway Administration.

- Americans rely on privately owned vehicles for 91.2 percent of all personal travel, according to the FHA.

Activities that divert your attention from the task at hand place you, your passengers and others on the road at risk. There are three types of distractions:

- Physical distractions cause you to take your hands off the wheel or eyes off the road. Examples are tuning a radio, reaching for a drink or dialing a mobile phone. Even a momentary distraction can cause you to run off the road or miss a traffic signal.

- Cognitive distractions take your mind off the road. Examples are having a conversation with a passenger, talking on a mobile phone or thinking about what to prepare for dinner. How many times have you had your eyes on the road but let your mind wander?

- Some activities take your hands, eyes and mind off driving. An example is reading a map.

Regardless of the reason, distractions impair a driver's ability. Impaired drivers react more slowly to traffic conditions or events, such as a car slowing to turn or pulling out from a side road; impaired drivers fail more often to recognize potential hazards, such as pedestrians, bicycles or road debris; impaired drivers decrease their margin of safety, leading them to take risks they might not otherwise take, such as turning left in front of oncoming traffic.

All are common factors in vehicle crashes. Driver focus is critical to anticipating and avoiding collisions.

Follow these tips for managing distractions:

- Recognize that driving requires your full attention. If your mind wanders, remind yourself to stay focused.

- Avoid talking on the phone while driving.

- If using a phone is unavoidable, use it at a safe time and place, keep the conversation short and postpone emotional or complex conversations until you are off the road.

- Avoid taking calls while driving. Use the message-taking function on your mobile phone and return calls when stopped at a safe location.

- Before you get behind the wheel, familiarize yourself with the features of your vehicle's equipment.

- Preset radio stations and climate control.

- Secure items that may move around when the car is in motion.

- Avoid smoking, eating, drinking and reading while driving.

- Pull safely off the road and out of traffic to deal with children.

- Do your personal grooming at home — not in the car.

- Review maps before hitting the road.

- Monitor traffic conditions before engaging in activities that could divert attention from driving.

- Ask a passenger to help you do the things that can be distracting.

Be Prepared for Anything

Night or day, curves and hills present additional problems. When approaching either, if you can't see all of the pavement you'll cover in the next four seconds, slow down. You need at least this much time to stop.

Rain, snow, ice, sand, wet leaves and oil slicks can impair your ability to stop, go and steer. If you think you're headed into an area of reduced traction, slow down and leave more space between your car and the vehicle in front of you.

Good risk managers never take to the road while impaired. In addition to being sober, you should be rested, healthy, emotionally stable and free of medications that affect your motor skills or your ability to concentrate. All can significantly reduce your ability to drive well and respond quickly and correctly to an emergency.

Use Caution in Work Zones

Nearly 800 fatal and more than 37,000 serious-injury crashes happen annually in work zones. Additionally, congestion and delays — and subsequently, driver frustration — are on the rise. The Federal Highway Administration offers several tips to help drivers stay safe in work zones:

- Stay alert. Dedicate your full attention to the roadway.

- Pay close attention to signs and work-zone flag men (or women).

- Turn on your headlights so workers and other motorists can see you easily.

- Don't tailgate.

- Don't speed. Obey the posted speed limits in and around the work zone.

- Keep up with the traffic flow.

- Don't change lanes.

- Minimize distractions. Don't change radio stations or use a mobile telephone while driving in the work zone.

Interpret the Other Driver's Behavior

Managing risk takes practice. You need to concentrate and implement good habits when you're behind the wheel. You have to think of what can go wrong and how you would react. If you're often unprepared when other drivers do something unexpected, you're not a risk manager. Your lack of a strategy for handling problems surrenders your safety into the hands of other drivers.

Managing risk means picking up clues to anticipate what other drivers might do. Unusual actions can be hints about what could happen next.

Drivers who slow or brake for no apparent reason may be confused, lost or looking for an address. Expect them to turn or stop suddenly.

Drivers often drift to one side of the lane before turning, even if the directional signal isn't blinking. Drivers who slow and drift toward the center of the road often turn left; those who slow and drift toward the curb often turn right. However, a few drivers drift away from a corner before they turn, just as the driver of a big truck would have to do. This dangerous cornering technique can be chalked up to laziness or the desire to increase the turning radius and reduce the feeling of being pulled to the outside of the corner.

Slow driving, weaving and stopping well before stop lines are all signs of an impaired motorist. If necessary, go out of your way to avoid this driver.

Because drivers tend to steer where they look, you can expect a motorist looking left or right to move in that direction.

Motorists who drive erratically, weave or significantly exceed the speed limit often are in a hurry. They could be impatient, late for an appointment or, in an extreme case, fleeing from a bank robbery. Let this driver pass, then keep your distance. That way, his problem won't become your problem.

The ability to anticipate is a powerful tool. It's what made Wayne Gretzky a phenomenal hockey player. Neither the fastest skater nor the most powerful on-ice athlete, Gretzky nonetheless became a hockey legend because he knew how to anticipate. "Other players go to where the puck is," he was once quoted as saying. "I go to where the puck will be." Anticipating the actions of other drivers and pedestrians will make you safer on every trip.

Chapter 3

Highway Driving

In This Chapter

• • • • • • • • • • • •

- How empty space can protect you

- How to cope with trucks

- How to use your eyes more effectively

- How to take the worry out of merging

After battling bumper-to-bumper traffic, you can't beat the feeling of getting out on a smooth, open highway. This is hardly a time to relax, however. Sadly, more than half of all traffic deaths occur in one-car crashes on relatively open roads.

Not all highways, of course, encourage a casual approach to driving. Some can be downright nasty. Narrow lanes, poor shoulders, inadequate grading, frequent intersections and limited sight lines conspire to make some two-lane and non-divided four-lane highways extremely dangerous. Limited-access highways tend to be much safer, but you still need to be careful.

Higher speeds make highway crashes more dangerous. More than half of all traffic deaths occur on roads with a speed limit of 55 mph or higher, even though less than half of the driving Americans do is on these roads. In contrast, drivers are more likely to sustain crash injuries on roads with a speed limit of 50 mph or less.

DID YOU KNOW? The color of pavement markings indicates the direction of traffic in other lanes. A yellow line to your left tells you traffic in the lane to your left will come toward you. A white line to your left means traffic in that lane should travel in your direction. Reflectors embedded in the roadway use yellow and white in a similar fashion to indicate traffic direction, but they also can reflect red to indicate you're driving the wrong way and blue to show the location of a fire hydrant.

Interstate Highways Are Safe

That noted, the safety of the nation's interstate highways is good. In 1998, the fatality rate on these roads was 0.87 deaths per 100 million vehicle-miles of travel, a unit measuring the mileage traveled by all vehicles. The rate for all roads in the national highway system was almost twice as high: 1.59 deaths per 100 million vehicle-miles of travel.

Therefore, driving on interstate highways is safer, despite the higher speeds. You usually can see ahead more easily on an interstate than on a city street. It's also easier to leave an appropriate cushion of space ahead of your vehicle and on at least one side, even on highways that pass through urban areas.

Interstate driving does present specific challenges though. Because you're driving faster, scanning 20 to 30 seconds ahead means looking a half-mile down the road. Keeping track of what's going on up to 15 seconds in front of you requires you to look at least a quarter-mile down the road.

In addition, other vehicles may come up quickly from the rear, you encounter more big trucks and, while there is no cross-traffic, you have to deal with drivers who want to merge onto or exit the highway, just as you have to do yourself.

Maintaining an adequate cushion of space around your vehicle is of utmost importance on highways where speeds are higher, largely because of the way vehicles stop. Each time your speed doubles, your stopping distance quadruples.

This can confuse beginning drivers who don't have enough experience to gauge how long it will take to stop a vehicle traveling at higher speeds. The longer distances may surprise even experienced drivers.

At highway speeds, increase the distance between your car and the vehicle in front from three seconds to four or five seconds. In addition, know where you can go if your lane suddenly becomes blocked.

Take weather into account when determining a safe speed and an adequate space cushion. Rain, snow and fog all can reduce both your ability to see and the ability of

SAFETY

Many of us learned to leave one car length of space between our vehicles and the car in front for every 10 mph — the equivalent of six car lengths at 60 mph. Unfortunately, this distance is woefully inadequate. For the average 15-foot car traveling 60 mph, this guideline would suggest a 90-foot gap, or just about one second. At the same speed, the "three-second rule" provides a 264-foot gap. Consider that an average driver traveling 60 mph in an average car under ideal circumstances takes about 230 feet to stop — 90 feet to perceive and react and 140 feet to come to a halt once the brakes are applied. It's obvious why the old rule should be discarded.

other drivers to see you. Slow down and leave more room around your car. If the weather also affects traction — as rain, snow, sleet and ice always do — expand the cushion of space even more. On ice and snow, you need eight to 10 seconds of space.

SAFETY Low-beam headlights may not make it easier for you to see in bad weather, but they do make it easier for other motorists to see you. Many states require you to use low beams when weather conditions force you to use your windshield wipers. Low-beam headlights also make your car easier to see on bright, sunny days. Using them on secondary roads can nearly double the distance at which oncoming drivers can see your car. Many fleet operators require the use of low beams all the time. Make it your rule as well.

Give Room to Big Rigs

On highways, you're likely to come into contact with more big trucks than you would on city streets. You'd be wise to be concerned — and alert. Logic should tell you that a 1.5-ton passenger car or two-ton compact sport-utility vehicle stands little chance in a collision with a 40-ton fully loaded tractor-trailer rig — or even a 15-ton empty one.

According to recent federal statistics, crashes between passenger cars and heavy trucks killed 1,905 car occupants and 33 people in heavy trucks — a ratio of 57 auto-passenger deaths for every fatality in a heavy truck. In crashes between light and heavy trucks, the ratio is 36-to-1 in favor of the heavy truck.

Large trucks play a critical role in the nation's economy and their numbers are likely to increase dramatically. The need to share the road safely has never been greater.

Heavy trucks require special consideration from car and light-truck drivers. Fully loaded big rigs need much more distance to stop than do passenger cars — about twice the distance from 60 mph. If a truck is on your bumper, you can't stop quickly if a problem ahead develops.

Here are some pointers on sharing the road safely with trucks:

- Give yourself ample time to pass a large truck. At highway speeds, it can take up to 30 seconds to do so safely. However, don't continuously drive beside a truck. If you do, you're in the trucker's blind spot. After passing, change lanes only when you can see the truck's headlights or front grille in your rearview mirror.

- Stay at least four seconds behind a big truck to keep out of the driver's rear blind spot. As the truck passes a stationary object beside the road, count to four. If your front bumper reaches the object before you reach "one thousand four," you're too close to the truck.

- Be aware of the driver's four blind spots or "no-zones." The front no-zone is 10 to 20 feet in front of the cab. The rear no-zone extends 200 feet behind — or two-

'No-Zones'

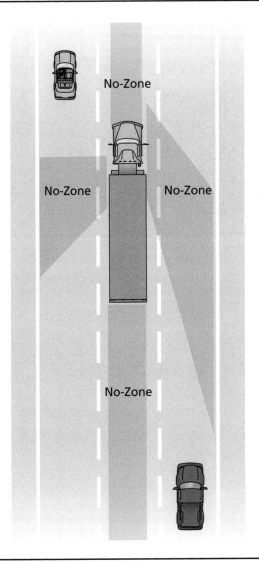

Unlike drivers of most passenger vehicles, truck drivers have four blind spots or "no-zones." Large blind spots extend down both sides of the truck, as well as 10 to 20 feet in front of it and 200 feet behind it.

Share with Care

The number of large trucks on the road is on the rise. Your passenger vehicle doesn't stand much of a chance in a collision with one, so you're wise to give big rigs plenty of space and special consideration.

thirds the length of a football field. Large blind spots, much larger than a car driver's blind spots, extend down both sides of the truck. Don't "hang out" on either side of a truck. If you're in one of the blind spots, you're in big trouble if that driver swerves or changes lanes.

- Trucks create wind gusts. Keep both hands on the wheel when you pass a truck or a truck passes you.

- Leave plenty of room between your vehicle and the back of a truck when stopping on an incline. Trucks may roll back as the driver releases the brake.

- Don't speed up when a truck passes you. Instead, stay to the right and slow down slightly. This gives the truck plenty of room to pass safely and gets you out of the blind spot faster.

- If a truck driver signals to change lanes, give him room. An average truck changing lanes at highway speeds needs an eight-second gap. That's equal to 700 feet — nearly three football fields.

Because of their weight, trucks are downright sluggish to handle. They accelerate slowly and their drivers often can't keep pace when climbing hills. To build momentum between hills, truck drivers may let their rigs gather speed on downhill sections of highway. In some cases, a mechanical failure may cause a runaway truck that can accelerate to twice the legal speed limit.

When descending long hills, constantly watch your rearview mirrors to make sure no trucks are gaining on you. If you see a truck approaching quickly, assume it is a

SAFETY Many states in hilly regions provide escape paths for runaway trucks Usually accessed from the highway's right lane, the paths go steeply uphill or into soft, deep sand — both of which quickly and safely stop a runaway truck. Because you never know when a truck driver will need to use this escape route, never park in front of the entrance to one.

runaway. Regardless of whether you see smoke rising from the brakes, the safest thing you can do is get out of the truck's way immediately.

Don't assume that if you can see the truck's mirrors, the driver will see you. Remember: The truck driver still has to look in the mirror.

On highways with three or more lanes going in the same direction, you might head for the center lanes, which often have a smoother flow of traffic away from vehicles entering and leaving the highway. However, in areas where trucks are banned from the far left lane, vehicles in the center obstruct the truck driver's only legal passing lane. If you're cruising along in the center lane and a truck is camped out on your bumper, pull to the right and let it pass.

Watch a truck's turn signals. Trucks make wide right turns. A truck may appear to be going straight or turning left when it's really making a right turn. This practice — combined with blind spots beside the trailer — makes trying to pass a turning truck a dangerous maneuver. Truck drivers can't see cars squeezing in between them and the curb. Stay put and give truckers plenty of room to turn.

Focus on What's Ahead of You

How you use your eyes on the highway affects your safety. On rural highways, not only must you look far ahead, you also have to be particularly aware of events taking place by the roadside. Slow-moving farm vehicles, livestock, wild animals, playing children and hidden driveways and side streets are common. In addition, rural railroad crossings often lack the warning lights or gates found at crossings in urban areas. More than 60 percent of railroad crossing fatalities happen in rural areas.

The challenges on urban highways are different. You encounter shopping center and mall entrances, school zones and home driveways, as well as pedestrians, bicyclists, joggers, pets and countless cars and trucks whose drivers are lost or who need to turn or stop.

Whether you drive on urban, suburban or rural highways, look far ahead, assess the possibility of dangerous situations and formulate plans for dealing with them.

Entering or crossing highways presents several problems. At the top of the list is the speed of traffic already on the highway. Unfortunately, the human eye is ill-equipped to judge the speed of an approaching vehicle, especially one that is more than a third of a mile away. Many people assume an oncoming car is going the speed limit. Unfortunately, not every approaching driver is so conscientious.

Many driving manuals suggest ways to determine whether you can cross safely in the face of oncoming traffic. Here's one technique to try: Don't drive in front of an oncoming vehicle unless you'd be willing to walk —

not run — in front of it to cross the same road. If you want to merge, wait for an even bigger gap in traffic. Accelerate quickly once you merge to reduce the likelihood of a vehicle striking you from behind.

Merge Cautiously

Merging into traffic on a limited-access highway presents other problems. On highways with an adequate entrance ramp, signal your intent to merge as you accelerate on the ramp and check traffic on the highway by looking over your shoulder. Before you near the end of the entrance ramp, check your mirrors and the view over your shoulder again to make sure you have enough room to enter the highway. If you don't, adjust your speed so you merge just as there is an adequate traffic gap to accommodate your vehicle. If you must slow, check your mirrors first to ensure that another merging motorist behind you isn't paying more attention to highway traffic than to what you're doing. Rarely does the entrance-ramp pavement end abruptly. If you don't have space to merge, use the paved shoulder to continue until you can safely merge rather than braking hard.

Weave lanes — lanes in which drivers merging onto the highway encounter other cars trying to leave on an approaching exit ramp — can be even more complicated. When entering on a weave lane, be especially alert. Expect exiting motorists to cut in front of you and brake, just as you want to accelerate. Generally, drivers on the entrance ramp should yield right of way to exiting drivers.

Weave Lane

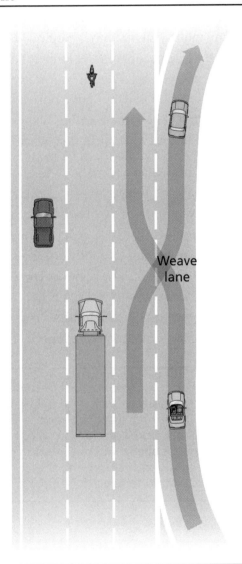

In a weave lane, drivers merging onto or exiting the highway share the same lane. If you're merging, prepare for an exiting motorist to cut in front of you and slow when you need to accelerate to enter traffic.

Exiting a non-divided highway — that is, a road without a median — can be another challenge. To exit left from many multi-lane roadways, you need to slow before the turn while occupying the lane usually reserved for faster traffic and passing. Watch your mirrors for an approaching driver who may not have noticed your brake lights or turn signal. The same warning is appropriate when you want to turn right off the roadway.

Leaving most limited-access roads — for example, interstate highways and freeways — is easier. Highway exit ramps usually enable you to clear the travel lane completely before slowing, which reduces the likelihood of being struck from behind. Nonetheless, pay close attention to the traffic behind whenever you change lanes or slow down. Recent statistics indicate that more than a million vehicles were involved in crashes triggered by a driver stopping or slowing in a traffic lane.

> **SAFETY** While you wait for oncoming traffic to clear before turning left, point your front tires straight ahead. If you are struck from behind, you will be pushed straight ahead and not into the path of oncoming traffic. Turn the tires left only after it is safe to begin the turn.

If the limited-access highway doesn't have a long enough exit ramp to let you start slowing after you leave the main traffic lanes, pay particularly close attention to traffic behind you as you slow while still on the road. Don't slow more than necessary, but make sure your speed drops enough for you to safely use the exit ramp.

If a driver behind you fails to notice that you are slowing and seems likely to hit you, abandon your plan to exit. Instead, accelerate to avoid the collision. Missing your exit is far better than being hit.

Use Care When Changing Lanes

Lane changes require extra caution. First, check your mirrors. If what you see indicates that you can safely change lanes, signal your intention, check your mirrors again, then look over your shoulder in the direction you plan to go to make sure no vehicle is hidden in your blind spot. If changing lanes on a multi-lane road, make sure no other motorist several lanes over is trying to occupy the spot where you want to move. If the way is clear, gently steer into the new lane then cancel your directional signal.

Always look over your shoulder before changing lanes. Mirrors don't show you everything you need to see. Some 345,000 vehicles crashed during simple lane changes, according to the most recent federal figures available.

> **DID YOU KNOW?**
>
> If you have difficulty turning your head to check blind spots before changing lanes, install additional mirrors. They're available from many auto parts stores as well as from companies that specialize in modifying vehicles for drivers with disabilities.

Be Fit to Drive

While you should be fit to drive every time you get behind the wheel, highway trips are often longer, making fatigue a common problem. To make sure you're ready, get adequate rest before starting out. Once on your way, stop every hour or two to rest and walk around the car. Avoid heavy meals, alcohol and temperature extremes, all of which can make you drowsy. Don't drive past your normal bedtime, and be aware of the lack of energy most people face in the afternoon. If another driver is with you, rotate time behind the wheel.

Driving Sport-Utility Vehicles and Pickups

In This Chapter

• • • • • • • • • • •

- What you should think about before driving a sport-utility vehicle or pickup

- How to load a vehicle

- Why some trucks are more likely than passenger cars to roll over

Truck makers reached a milestone in 2001 — it was the first year in which more Americans bought new trucks than new cars. The margin of victory for trucks was small, but that it happened at all is surprising when you consider that trucks accounted for only one-third of new-vehicle sales just a decade earlier.

Contributing to the sales tallies are government and automobile industry definitions that put the "truck" label on pickups, sport-utility vehicles, full-size vans, minivans and some other vehicles most people probably think of as cars. Insurance industry definitions, however, often place minivans in the "passenger car" category.

Find the Truck

COURTESY OF HONDA, DODGE, NISSAN, CHRYSLER

Government and automobile industry definitions attach the "truck" label to pickups, as well as sport-utility vehicles, minivans and even the Chrysler PT Cruiser.

DID YOU KNOW? The difference between a car and a truck is more than academic. More stringent safety requirements apply to passenger cars, and weaker environmental standards — both in terms of fuel efficiency and emissions — apply to trucks.

Bigger Isn't Always Better

Many people buy trucks not for their utility but for their perceived safety. This assumption's validity is questionable.

Most trucks are big and heavy, factors many buyers equate with safety. Many trucks also seat drivers higher off the ground, which gives them a better view of the road ahead — another safety benefit. But trucks handle differently from cars, and failing to appreciate those differences can lead to serious consequences.

Size and weight definitely affect vehicle safety in a crash. In one sense, bigger is always better because more of the vehicle can collapse in a controlled manner during a collision. Controlled deformation of the engine and luggage compartments reduces the crash stresses that can injure or kill the vehicle's occupants.

Because bigger vehicles also are heavier, it's difficult to separate the effect of size from weight when studying crash statistics. In two-vehicle crashes, the heavier vehicle almost always sustains less damage. However, in a

> **SAFETY** Despite their big, strong image, some trucks don't do well in crash tests. A few have fared particularly poorly in the Insurance Institute for Highway Safety's offset barrier crash test. While many manufacturers object to this test because of its severity — research shows the vast majority of real-world crashes are less demanding on a vehicle's structure — some trucks have performed well in it. If crash-test safety is important to you, check results from both the National Highway Traffic Safety Administration at www.nhtsa.gov and the IIHS at www.hwysafety.org.

single-vehicle crash with a stationary object such as a bridge abutment, additional weight may be a detriment as it adds to the forces that must be managed by the body structure.

Generally, insurance industry loss data show that occupants of bigger, heavier vehicles fare better in most crashes than occupants in smaller, lighter vehicles. However, even within size and weight classes, insurance industry figures suggest that some vehicles are much safer than others.

> **PITFALLS**
>
> Although driver death rates for 1994-97 model year vehicles were mostly consistent within weight and vehicle categories, the Insurance Institute for Highway Safety has noted significant exceptions. The Honda Civic stands out in its class with a death rate of less than half that of the Nissan Sentra, less than two-fifths that of the Geo Prizm and Dodge/Plymouth Neon and less than one-third that of the former Kia Sephia, now the Spectra. These differences may reflect the vehicle's target market — in other words, some cars appeal to drivers who take more risks — or handling differences that help drivers avoid crashes.

Rollover Rates Are Higher

Insurance statistics also show that other factors hinder passenger safety in truck crashes. "Within any given weight class, pickup trucks have the highest driver death rates, and four-wheel-drive pickups are the worst," the Insurance Institute for Highway Safety noted in a status report addressing driver death rates. "High single-vehicle rollover death rates are major contributors to the poor overall rates in these vehicles."

Although rollovers occur in only 2.6 percent of all crashes, they often are deadly. Rollovers factored in 15.3 percent of the deaths in passenger vehicles, 24.3 percent of deaths in pickups and 36.3 percent of deaths in crashes of sport-utility vehicles, according to the most recent federal figures.

Insurance Institute for Highway Safety-Highway Loss Data Institute numbers also indicate that people in trucks are more likely to die in single-vehicle rollover crashes than are people in cars. In single-vehicle crashes, rollovers factored in 11 percent of passenger deaths in large cars and 22 percent of deaths in small cars. Compare that to a 51 percent rollover death rate for passengers in small trucks and small four-wheel-drive sport-utility vehicles, a 48 percent death rate in large pickups and a startling 59 percent death rate in large SUVs.

SAFETY Rollover crashes often are deadly because passengers can be ejected. Being thrown from a vehicle rarely helps you, so wearing a seat belt is critical to your safety. Some 1,300 of 8,000 people who died after being thrown from a vehicle could have been saved had they remained inside, according to estimates from some automobile industry trade groups.

Several factors make trucks more likely than cars to roll in a crash. For starters, there's the high center of gravity, a byproduct of the need to design a vehicle that, when equipped with four-wheel drive, can tackle rough off-road conditions. Manufacturers must raise the vehicle so it can clear stumps and rocks and limit its width so it can handle tight clearances found in the wild. Making a vehicle higher and narrower also makes it easier to roll over.

Centers of Gravity

Because they are higher than passenger cars, sport-utility vehicles have a higher center of gravity. This makes them more likely to roll over.

   That few SUV drivers ever deliberately leave the urban jungle doesn't matter. If advertisers promise a credible off-road performance, these vehicles must deliver.

Because few sport-utility vehicle drivers ever venture into the wild, the automobile industry is marketing crossover vehicles. They resemble traditional SUVs but can't tackle rugged off-road conditions. These vehicles, such as the Ford Escape, Honda CR-V and Toyota RAV4, often are based on passenger-car structures and usually ride and handle better, cost less and get better fuel economy than their truck-based brethren.

Drive Trucks Within Safe Limits

When driving a truck with a high center of gravity, modify your driving style. Slow down when you take corners to reduce the centrifugal force that can lead to rollovers.

Thrill-seekers aside, most motorists don't exceed their vehicle's safe handling limits when cornering. In an emergency, however, all bets are off. Turning maneuvers that are easy in a sports sedan can be deadly in a truck. If you take a corner too quickly, most vehicles — including sport-utility vehicles, large vans and pickup trucks — will skid sideways. If the tires suddenly bite or hit a pothole or curb during the slide, the vehicle can trip and roll over.

Some trucks and SUVs also can roll without skidding first. All it takes is swerving quickly one way to avoid an obstacle, then steering just as quickly in the other direction to stay on the road. This steering sequence causes the body to sway first to one side and then the other, much as an upside-down pendulum would. On the return swing, the body gathers the momentum to push the vehicle over. While this can happen even when the vehicle is empty, a full load boosts the likelihood of rolling.

DID YOU KNOW?	Stability enhancement systems can significantly reduce the likelihood of vehicle rollover. By helping a driver prevent a skid, they cut down the chances of a crash or of rolling over after tripping on a pothole, curb or other obstacle.

Carry Cargo Carefully

Load heavier items lower and farther forward in the cargo area. In a sport-utility vehicle or pickup truck, move items ahead of the rear axle and keep them on the floor, if possible. Placing heavy items behind the rear axle will adversely affect handling. Raising the load off the floor will affect stability in corners.

Increased Rollover Risk

Adding passengers and cargo to a sport-utility vehicle raises its center of gravity and increases the risk of rolling. If you must use the roof rack, pay attention to the manufacturer's weight limit.

Avoid using a roof rack. But if you must, heed the manufacturer's weight limits, which are often just 175 or 200 pounds. While the roof rack might be able to hold more, the maker's recommendation is based on how the vehicle handles when loaded and how much weight the roof sheet metal can support. Remember: Adding passengers and cargo can raise the center of gravity.

Cargo Distribution

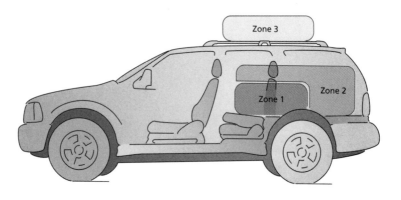

When loading a sport-utility vehicle, fold down the back seats and place items lower and farther forward in the zone 1 space of the cargo area. Loading cargo in zones 2 and 3 will adversely affect handling.

All vehicles have a maximum cargo capacity. Even a heavy-duty truck can easily be overloaded. Just because an item fits in the truck doesn't mean you can carry it safely. To find out how much your car or truck can carry, check the owner's manual.

For an older vehicle, you'll probably see a single figure: the GVWR, or gross vehicle weight rating. This number represents what the vehicle and its cargo — including passengers — can weigh. To determine the cargo capacity, subtract the vehicle weight from the GVWR. Because some owner's manuals don't list vehicle weight, you may have to check the shop manual, call the dealer or manufacturer or even have the vehicle weighed. Fortunately, makers of newer vehicles are beginning to disclose cargo weight limits clearly in manuals.

Vehicle weight and cargo capacity vary depending on the model and optional equipment. If you ordered many options, each one that added weight probably reduced your cargo capacity. Ordering four-wheel drive can take several hundred pounds off the cargo capacity. In the same way, a bigger engine may actually reduce the load you can carry, despite its added power. Even beefy-looking trucks and sport-utility vehicles can have a surprisingly low cargo capacity. Some sport-utility vehicles can carry only 1,000 pounds before exceeding their GVWR.

SAFETY One often-overlooked aspect of a vehicle's carrying capacity is tire pressure. Inflate tires to the maximum pressure specified by the vehicle manufacturer. This is almost always lower than the maximum figure stamped on the tire's sidewall. Letting tire pressure drop below the manufacturer's recommendation significantly reduces the load-carrying capacity and increases the potential for tire failure.

Know What Your Truck Can Tow Safely

Although some truck makers boast of impressive trailer-towing ratings, not all models they make can tow that weight. Trucks often require optional equipment to tow heavier trailers and, in many cases, the trailer will need its own brakes. Pay close attention to the tongue weight rating — the downward pressure, measured in pounds, that the trailer hitch can safely place on the vehicle. You'll also need a properly attached trailer hitch.

Exceeding the manufacturer's maximum load recommendation, either in cargo or from a trailer, may make the vehicle difficult to stop, turn or accelerate. It also can shorten the life of chassis components, such as wheel bearings, tires, axles and the drivetrain. A sudden failure of these parts could kill you.

Many trucks handle more sluggishly than cars and take longer to stop, even when empty. Data published in the *AAA Auto Guide: New Cars and Trucks* show that compared to cars, trucks take roughly a car length longer to stop — and sometimes as long as three car lengths — from 60 mph. This can mean the difference between stopping in time and having a major — or even fatal — crash.

Don't Put Passengers in Cargo Bed

Some pickup drivers foolishly carry passengers or pets in the cargo bed. Completely unprotected, they can be thrown from the bed and, if the pickup rolled over, could be crushed.

A person riding in a truck's cargo bed is three times more likely to die in a crash than a person in the cab. Approximately 200 people are killed and thousands more are injured each year when riding in truck cargo beds.

While 29 states and the District of Columbia restrict riding in a truck's cargo bed, smart passengers don't do it even where it's legal.

In addition, never install a child-safety seat in a pickup truck's jump seat. Jump seats aren't sufficiently stable and you'd be putting your child and everyone else in the cab at risk.

Safety boils down to the driver, the vehicle and the road. Recognizing the operating parameters of all three can greatly increase your safety.

Chapter 5

Avoiding and Handling Crashes

In This Chapter

• • • • • • • • • • • •

- How small changes in speed can have a major effect on your risk

- How to handle skids

- What to do after a crash

- Why you should get the police involved after a crash

- Tips on getting your car back on the road

Your chances of crashing your vehicle in the next year are between one in five and one in 10. Those aren't good odds.

It's difficult to determine how many crashes occur each year. Many people handle minor fender-benders and even more serious accidents without involving either the police or their insurance company. While that may be appealing, it's also risky. Seemingly minor crashes can lead to litigation for substantial sums, and if you don't promptly inform your insurance carrier that you were involved in the crash, you may place your coverage at risk.

Obviously, the best way to handle a crash is to avoid it. The techniques outlined in Chapter 2 should help you do that. Sometimes, however, you will still find yourself in trouble, even after doing everything right. Knowing what to do in an emergency can save your life.

More than one-third of all drivers who crash do nothing to prevent it, according to AAA driver-improvement program statistics. They don't brake, swerve or accelerate, and the older they are, the more likely they are to do nothing just before crashing.

The good news is that two-thirds of crash victims tried to avoid the collision. Unfortunately, they either didn't act in time or did something wrong.

Surviving a Close Call

In most emergencies, motorists escape either by doing something right or coming across another driver who acts appropriately. How many near-misses happen every year? No one knows, but the number must be staggering. If you've spent any time behind the wheel, you can probably recall plenty.

Handling emergencies properly is vital to your driving survival. Taking the right action at the right time in a difficult situation requires knowledge, composure under pressure, practice in emergency avoidance and good luck. Don't put too much stock in luck. After one of his better tournament rounds, golfer Gary Player told an interviewer who commented on his good luck, "The more I practice, the luckier I get." The same holds true for drivers.

Close calls happen for many reasons. Among the most common are inattention and distractions. Inattention is when your mind wanders. Distractions are actions or events inside or outside the vehicle that draw your concentration away from driving.

Prepare for Emergencies

To handle emergencies properly, you must know how your vehicle is equipped and how it will respond. Instructors no longer are surprised when the majority of people in driver-improvement programs don't know whether their vehicle has antilock brakes, stability enhancement or even an air bag. Each affects how you should operate your vehicle and what you should do in an emergency.

Keep the Air Bag in Mind When Steering

Depending on how you hold and use the steering wheel and how close to it you sit, the rapid, forceful deployment of an air bag can save your life or inflict severe injuries.

Most drivers were trained to use hand-over-hand steering. To turn a corner using this method, your hands constantly cross each other and your arms often form an "x" over the air bag. If you were to crash in the middle of a turn, the air bag could severely injure your arms and hands, perhaps even pushing them into your body or head with significant force.

Developed when steering wheels were large, power steering was unknown, and turning from left to right took six or more revolutions of the steering wheel, hand-over-hand steering has outlived its usefulness. The advent of more responsive power steering and smaller steering wheels prompted driving experts to reconsider hand-over-hand steering even before air bags debuted. In its place, they developed push-pull-slide steering. Air bags make it even more important to adopt this method.

To use push-pull-slide steering, imagine the steering wheel is a clock face. Grasp the wheel with your left hand at the 7 to 8 o'clock position, and place your right hand at the 4 to 5 o'clock position. This is your normal driving posture.

This is how you'd make a right turn.

1. Grasp the wheel firmly with your left hand and loosen your right hand's grip so the wheel will slide through your right hand.

2. Raise both hands up the wheel so your left hand, which is firmly grasping the wheel, goes to the 10 or 11 o'clock position. That will turn the wheel to the right. At the same time, your right hand will move to the corresponding 1 or 2 o'clock position while the wheel slides through your right fingers.

3. If you need to turn the wheel more, grasp it firmly with your raised right hand and pull it down. Simultaneously, loosen your left hand's grip on the wheel and slide this hand down over the moving wheel, letting it remain at the same height as your right hand.

4. If necessary, repeat the procedure.

At no time will either hand cross the wheel's 12 o'clock position. To turn the wheel left, reverse the hands that grasp and slide.

Push-Pull-Slide Steering

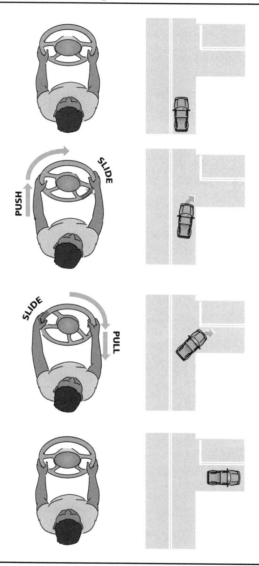

Developed because of more responsive steering and smaller steering wheels, push-pull-slide steering is much preferred to hand-over-hand steering because it keeps arms out of the way of the air bag if it deploys.

This technique keeps your arms from crossing in front of the air bag. It also reduces the role your shoulders play in steering maneuvers, which in turn limits the likelihood you will overreact in an emergency and steer off the road by mistake. This is especially important in cars with antilock brakes, which allow a driver to steer during emergency stops. Insurance industry statistics have shown that many drivers with these brakes end up crashing after steering off the road.

DID YOU KNOW? Even if you've adopted new techniques such as push-pull-slide steering, it's common to revert to old behaviors in an emergency. It takes a long time for any new behavior to become second nature in a difficult situation. So practice, practice, practice.

How Antilock Brakes Work

Increasingly common as either standard or optional equipment, antilock braking systems help keep tires rotating when you stop on a slippery surface or when you slam on the brakes in an emergency. Because the tires never fully lock in an ABS-equipped vehicle, you maintain the ability to steer. In a vehicle without ABS, you lose the ability to steer the minute you lock the front tires. If the rear tires lock first, the car will skid and perhaps even spin.

To use antilock brakes properly, apply the brakes and steer as necessary. Don't pump the brakes. This defeats the system and lengthens your stopping distance. Don't steer too much, either. The lower hand position on the steering wheel lets you steer more precisely.

If your vehicle is equipped with antilock brakes, it may have an ABS symbol on the trunk lid, the wheels or the brake pedal, and all ABS-equipped vehicles have an ABS warning light on the instrument panel. It should light when you start your vehicle and then go out after a few seconds. If it stays on or comes on while you are driving, you've lost ABS protection, although your regular brakes should work normally. Have your vehicle checked at once.

SAFETY Cars have a four-wheel antilock braking system. On trucks the system can work either on all four wheels or just the rear ones. Four-wheel ABS is far better. In a two-wheel system, you still could lock the front tires and lose steering. To regain control, modulate your pressure on the brake pedal.

Capitalize on Stability Enhancement Systems

Once available only on expensive luxury cars, stability enhancement systems have worked their way into vehicles most buyers can afford. These systems detect a skid, often before the driver is even aware of the problem, and then help the driver keep the car under control.

DID YOU KNOW? Many stability enhancement systems can be turned off, but there are few good reasons to do so. Vehicles often are designed to override deactivated systems when the brakes are applied.

They work well, especially in emergency maneuvers. If your car or truck has stability enhancement, don't hesitate to turn during an emergency. While these systems won't repeal the laws of physics, they make it possible for you to maintain control during maneuvers that otherwise could result in a skid.

Electronic Stability Program

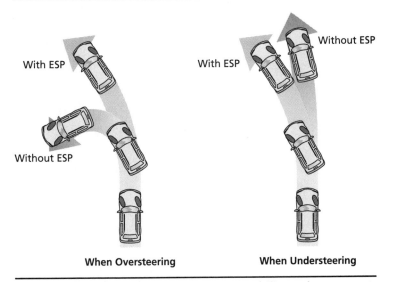

With ESP

Without ESP

Without ESP

With ESP

When Oversteering   **When Understeering**

Particularly in emergency maneuvers, stability enhancement systems can detect a skid and help you maintain control of the vehicle.

Knowing how your car is equipped is just the first step. You also must know how antilock braking and stability enhancement work on the road. Learning how to handle these systems requires practice. Find an empty parking lot with a slippery surface, such as sand, water or fresh snow, and no light poles or other obstructions.

First, stop quickly while going straight to activate the antilock braking system. Then experiment with steering while braking with the ABS on. If your car has stability enhancement, try a few quick turns back and forth to learn what the system will and won't do. No fire chief would let an untrained firefighter rush into a burning building, yet motorists who have never used their vehicle's ABS and stability enhancement features believe they can use them successfully in an emergency without a single practice session.

Many drivers of cars with antilock brakes believe the feature will decrease their stopping distance. It might, but there are no guarantees. Don't count on ABS to stop your car any faster than regular brakes. ABS-equipped vehicles can even take longer to stop than non-equipped vehicles on surfaces such as gravel roads. In addition, different vehicles will have different stopping distances under identical conditions.

In most emergencies, you'll have two options: Change your speed or change your direction. At slower speeds, it's almost always faster to stop. At speeds less than 30 or 35 mph, you should be able to stop faster than you can turn.

Stopping Distances

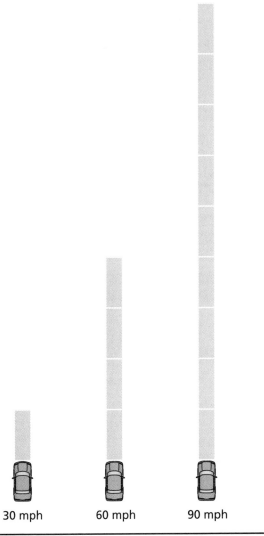

| 30 mph | 60 mph | 90 mph |

Doubling your speed doesn't mean you need just twice as much stopping distance. In fact, a vehicle traveling 60 mph will need **four** times as much stopping distance as a vehicle traveling 30 mph, and one traveling 90 mph will need **nine** times the distance.

On the highway at 60 mph, however, you probably can change lanes quicker than you can bring your car to a halt. Always know what's behind you and consider using an escape path in an emergency if you're not sure you can stop in time.

Dealing with Common Worries

Maintain Traction

Surfaces with sand, gravel, rain, snow or ice all rob your tires of the bite they would have on dry concrete or asphalt. Drive gently in reduced-traction conditions. Pretend you have a full, uncovered cup of coffee in the cup holder, then drive so you wouldn't spill a drop. Start, stop and turn smoothly. A soft touch on the steering wheel, accelerator and brake should prevent you from skidding in low-traction conditions.

Cope with a Skid

Short of crashing, few events strike more fear in drivers' hearts than skidding. The loss of control often feels complete, but usually isn't. With mental preparation and practice, you can handle any skid you can't avoid. Follow this simple, four-step approach:

1. Gently take your foot off the gas and keep it off the brake.

2. Look where you want to go.

3. Steer to get there.

> **SAFETY**
> You may have learned to steer in the direction the vehicle's rear end slips. This is correct, but it's hard to do intuitively. If you can train yourself to follow the four-step skid-handling approach, you'll end up steering into the skid.

4. If your first steering correction doesn't do the trick, don't give up. Keep trying to regain control, continue to look where you want to go and steer to get there.

Fishtailing on a slippery surface occurs mostly in rear-wheel-drive vehicles. Although it's possible in front-wheel-drive vehicles, it's less likely than having the vehicle plow nose-first toward the outside of a corner.

Correcting a Skid

If your vehicle's rear end slips, gently lift your foot from the accelerator, look where you want to go, steer to get there and keep trying to regain control.

Stop in an Emergency

With antilock braking systems, you simply slam on the brake to stop in an emergency. Without ABS, the process is more complex.

The goal is to apply enough pressure to bring your tires to the verge of locking without stopping them from rotating. This is hard to do, even for trained professionals. Chances are that you will apply too much pressure and lock one or more of the wheels in an emergency stop. When this happens, back off the brake just enough to let the tires start turning again, but not so much that your foot comes completely off the pedal.

Practice this emergency stopping technique on a vacant road with no other drivers in sight. When you first slam on the brakes, the car's front goes down, often referred to as the "nose dive." You can see the car's hood sink in relationship to the horizon. Once you lock a wheel, back off the brake enough to let the locked wheel begin rotating again, but not so much that the car's hood rises significantly. Once the locked wheel is turning again — you can feel it in the way the car responds and you can hear when the tires stop screeching — press a little harder on the brake until one or more wheels lock again so you can repeat the process. To exercise the fine control you need to control the brakes, keep your heel on the floor and press the brake with your toes rather than the ball of your foot.

Braking properly takes skill and practice. Drivers who do this well can keep the wheels right on the threshold of locking. They may even be able to stop in a shorter distance than the driver of an ABS-equipped vehicle.

> **DID YOU KNOW?** Several years ago, studies showed that a significant number of drivers failed to stomp the brake as hard as they should in an emergency. In a few cases, drivers lacked the strength. In others, improper seat adjustment kept them from pressing the brake over its full range of motion. In most cases, however, they simply lacked the will, even in the face of an emergency. These failures could add 100 feet to stopping distances at highway speeds.

When You Can't Avoid a Crash

When all of the above techniques fail, you may well crash. Most crashes are fender-benders, resulting only in property damage. Others, unfortunately, are more serious. Be prepared for either eventuality. Here's what you should do in a crash:

- Keep calm.

- Don't leave the scene unless your medical condition requires it.

- Assess the situation. Are there hazards such as passing traffic or downed power lines that you must avoid? Is any car leaking fluids? Whatever you do, stay off the traveled portion of the highway as you assess the crash scene.

- If you can do so safely, comfort the injured. Don't move any victim unless not doing so would result in more serious injuries or death. Don't administer first aid beyond your capabilities and don't offer drinking water to any injured person.

- Be sure the ignition switches of all significantly damaged cars are turned off.

- Don't move vehicles unless you must for safety or state law requires it.

- Set out warning triangles or flares to alert approaching traffic. On the highway, place the first warning device at least 300 feet back from the crash scene.

- Notify authorities.

- Gather information. Your insurance company may have a list of what you need, which undoubtedly includes the names and addresses of every person in the involved vehicles. Record the state and driver's license number of all operators, as well as each vehicle's make, model year, color, license plate number and 17-character vehicle identification number, or VIN.

- Summarize the crash damage and other damage the cars may have had before the collision. If you back into a vehicle's right front fender in a parking lot, note any unrelated damage elsewhere on the vehicle. An unscrupulous victim may attempt to package it all for a bigger settlement.

- Tell police the truth, but don't make judgments as to the accident's cause or who is at fault. You're probably rattled and might not know all the facts.

- Do the paperwork. Many states, as well as your insurance company, require written reports after a crash. Fill out the forms as soon as possible, while the events are fresh in your mind. Keep copies of everything you file.

While most police departments mandate that you leave vehicles where they are for the investigators, some jurisdictions require you to move them out of the way of traffic in certain circumstances. Moving vehicles may depend on whether the crash caused personal injuries or on the type of road where the accident occurred. Check your local laws to determine what you should do before you need to know.

Keep Supplies in the Car

To gather facts after the crash, you need a written list of the information to record, a working pen and a notebook in your car. A disposable camera lets you record the actual damage, the people involved and the vehicles' locations after the crash, as well as the weather and lighting conditions at the time of the incident.

Keep an emergency kit in your trunk. It should contain:

- Jumper cables
- A working flashlight with good batteries

Emergency Kit

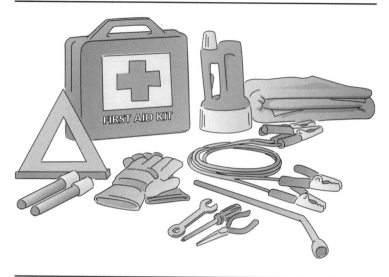

A well-stocked emergency kit should be kept in your vehicle's trunk, as should a blanket. Other items to have handy include a pen, notebook and disposable camera.

- Warning triangles or flares

- Basic hand tools

- T-wrench

- A first-aid kit

- Gloves and protective clothing

While not common in emergency kits, you should also carry a blanket, even in warm climates. Not only can you use it as a pillow, it also can protect an injured person from rain or cover a trapped crash victim while emergency workers cut apart metal and glass.

In areas where snow is common, add to your list a shovel, traction enhancer such as sand or clay cat litter, ice scraper and a small supply of non-perishable food. A cellular telephone also can be a lifesaver.

If you are involved in a crash that appears to be your fault, don't skip calling the police, especially if the other party doesn't want the authorities involved. Some criminals make a living by forcing innocent motorists to crash and then collecting large settlements from their insurance policies. Calling the police creates an official record of the event. It establishes a verifiable list of the people involved, events leading up to the crash and damage to the vehicles.

Be suspicious if the other party sees no reason to get the police involved, doesn't want to get you into trouble, prefers to work it out without paperwork or comes up with other excuses to avoid calling the authorities. This person may plan to hit you later with large claims for injuries and property damage. A police report would only complicate his life.

For most people who crash, an automotive repair shop writes the final chapter. Fortunately, people needing help can look to AAA for guidance. The Approved Auto Repair program can point you to repair shops known for providing high-quality service. These shops offer AAA members additional benefits, including accepting AAA arbitration in the unlikely event that you have a problem with the service. AAR garages agree to be bound by

AAA's findings in dispute resolution, while you, as a member, are free to accept or reject the finding. In some areas, AAA also has an Approved Auto Body Repair program, which reviews the work of automobile body and collision repair shops.

Some safety systems — such as seat sensors that provide information for air bag computers and bumpers hidden by flexible covers — may not readily show damage from a collision. Even if your car seems to have minimal damage, have it thoroughly checked by a skilled technician before returning it to the road.

Also, replace child-safety seats and consider replacing seat belts after a crash. The webbed material from which seat belts are made often stretches in a crash to absorb the energy of your forward-moving body. This compromises its integrity. Many insurance companies cover such replacements as needed repairs.

CHAPTER 6

Coping with Road Rage

In This Chapter

• • • • • • • • • • • •

- How to manage your anger

- How to avoid unnecessarily angering other motorists

- What leads to anger and rage

- Tips for avoiding or managing rage in others

With the release of its 1997 report *Aggressive Driving: Three Studies*, the AAA Foundation for Traffic Safety focused the nation's attention on a problem that, in the seven preceding years, had claimed more than 10,000 lives.

Aggressive driving, also called "road rage" by the media and one of the report's contributors, can happen to anyone. Given adequate provocation, no one is immune to becoming angry. At the same time, you can provoke that emotion in others, often without realizing it.

On the road, anger can result in tragic consequences. It can cloud judgment, disrupt thinking and erode maturity. Based on statistics in the foundation's report, approximately 3 percent of roadway fatalities happen as the result of driving under the influence of rage, with more grievous examples receiving ample media coverage.

Tragic Consequences

A California judge sentences 27-year-old telephone repairman Andrew Burnett to three years in prison for cruelty to animals — the maximum allowed under state law. The incident starts when Burnett cuts off another driver, Sara McBurnett, on a rain-soaked highway. She bumps Burnett's vehicle, prompting him to get out and, according to witnesses, charge over to her car in a state of rage. He then reaches through McBurnett's open window, grabs her lap dog and throws him into freeway traffic, where he is struck and killed.

In another incident in the Washington, D.C. area, Narkey Keval Terry, provoked by Billy Canipe's unwillingness to let him pass, began racing Canipe up the George Washington Parkway. Speeds hit 80 mph before their two cars crossed the median and hit two oncoming cars. Three of the four drivers died. Terry, the only survivor, was sentenced to 10 years in prison.

There's more to road rage than tragedies. It has become a backdrop for much of the daily driving you do, and it's not confined to the United States. The problem is worldwide.

Road Rage Consequences

Another vehicle was thought to have been chasing the two women who died in this road rage crash. Managing anger is key to preventing aggressive driving incidents.

In a survey included in the foundation's report, contributor Matthew Joint noted that almost 90 percent of motorists polled in Great Britain reported having been the object of another motorist's rage in the past year. Sixty percent also admitted to losing their temper while driving and subjecting another motorist to abusive treatment.

Closer to home and with the passage of time, the problem seems to be no less severe. In a recent poll funded by the Pew Charitable Trusts, 58 percent of U.S. respondents said they frequently encounter reckless, aggressive drivers on the road, and nearly two-thirds say the problem is getting worse.

Self-control can lapse from time to time. Ask teens learning to drive whether they threw or broke something out of anger or frustration in the past year, and nearly all admit that they have. But aggressive driving doesn't discriminate: There are ample reports of road rage by persons of both sexes and all ages.

> **PITFALLS**
>
> One theory suggests that letting frustrated individuals vent — to express or release their pent-up resentment — will quickly exhaust their anger. As they run out of steam, the theory goes, they'll realize the petty basis for their complaints and their excessive response. Calm is far from guaranteed. For some people, venting adds fuel to the fire. Instead of assuming that an angry motorist will regain control, get away from him or her.

Imagine the greater impact these people could have when, instead of throwing a 6-ounce coffee mug, they can hurl 3,500 pounds of steel, plastic, glass and rubber at 65 mph in the direction of the object of their displeasure. A body of evidence even links the popularity of big, heavy trucks to drivers' fears of "being pushed around" on the road.

Keep Your Cool

The only driver you can keep from becoming enraged is you.

Self-control is the key to preventing involvement in road-rage incidents. When provoked, don't respond. Anger is a learned behavior. If you become angry over minor issues, learn a less volatile way to deal with them.

Who hasn't accidentally cut off another driver or forgotten to dim high-beam headlights? When these things happen to you, give the other driver the benefit of the doubt. Don't assume it was deliberate, and don't take retaliatory action.

When you come across a driver who deliberately inconveniences you, don't react. Taking the bait and responding in kind serves only to escalate the conflict and risk. Retaliating drivers have ended up wounded, disabled and dead. Others now sit in prison, where they have ample time to regret losing their temper and inflicting injury or even killing someone. This is far too high a price to pay for shaving 30 seconds off your trip to the supermarket.

Many angry drivers start by being frustrated. If frustration leads you to anger, reduce irritants while you drive. Make your car more comfortable by adjusting the climate controls or playing soothing music. Don't think about events or listen to radio programs or music that make you angry.

If traffic bothers you, either accept that you can't change it or alter your schedule or route to avoid it. Leaving earlier or later often lets you bypass heavy traffic in urban areas. Plan longer trips so you won't drive through crowded cities during rush hour.

If, despite these efforts, you still become angry, get off the road and cool down. Relax for a few minutes before returning to the roadway. Never drive when you're angry about an incident unrelated to traffic. Inevitably, that anger will affect your driving. Remember that many disputes with tragic consequences are trivial — no matter how important they seemed at the time.

SAFETY There's no point in letting problems you can't control, including traffic, make you angry. Some people even suggest that traffic isn't a problem, but rather a condition, much like the sun setting tonight and rising again tomorrow. First, learn to accept traffic. Then do the same for motorists who make mistakes and even people who drive with needless aggression.

Prevention Is the Best Cure

Because the issues that trigger road rage in others and perhaps in yourself are most often trifling, you can take steps to avoid becoming a road-rage casualty.

Be Polite

Shielded by vehicles and partially hidden behind tinted windows, some drivers do things they would never do to another person face to face. Good manners on the road go a long way toward defusing potential conflicts. When in doubt, yield.

Leave Early

It's no surprise that lack of time, fear of being late and traffic delays don't mix. When you know you have an extra five minutes, missing a light because the driver ahead of you is slower than you like is no big deal.

Don't Tailgate

Impatient drivers often tailgate to get the driver in front to go faster. Don't do it. You risk a rear-end collision. Besides, drivers with passive-aggressive personalities will take great pleasure in slowing you down.

Let Tailgaters Pass

Some tailgaters are selfish; others are always running late. That seems harmless enough, but can you be sure that the next guy who gets too close to your rear bumper didn't just commit a crime with the arsenal of weapons in his trunk? To be safe, let tailgaters pass. Few recorded incidents of road rage are directed at the driver to the rear. (Just remember to dim your high beams at night when following another vehicle, and don't become a tailgater yourself.) Enraged motorists tend to direct their rage at the driver in front of them.

Don't Be a Left-Lane Bandit

Camping out in the left lane — the passing lane — and making others pass on the right is not only dangerous and often illegal, but also can provoke many generally sane motorists to anger. Even if you're going the speed limit, change lanes.

Signal Your Intentions

Use your directional signals and check your mirrors before changing direction or lanes: Many road-rage incidents start when one driver cuts off another. By

---

DID YOU KNOW?

Drivers often assume people who want to pass are rushing without good reason. "Let 'em wait," some drivers say. "I'm going as fast as is safe" is another common attitude. However, one couple came away with a different view. After rushing their infant daughter, who was having trouble breathing, to the hospital when no ambulance was available, the father said, "You have no idea how many people, seeing us coming up on them quickly, went out of their way to get in our way." That quickly approaching driver may have a legitimate reason for speed. Would you want to be blocked under such circumstances?

signaling, checking your mirrors and glancing over your shoulder before moving over, you can eliminate this problem.

Park with Care

Don't cut off another driver in your zeal to take the last parking spot in sight. Be careful when opening your door so you don't ding the side of the adjacent car. Also, when leaving a parking space in a crowded lot, don't dawdle. If challenged while parking, yield. You'll live to park another day. In the same vein, be careful when you see a line of motorists waiting to refuel at a gasoline station. A sudden pump opening can lead to a maneuvering frenzy you should avoid.

DID YOU KNOW? Before being angered by a driver who changes lanes without signaling, consider that it's possible that he or she did try to signal but the device failed to work correctly.

Don't Gesture to Show Displeasure

As the AAA Foundation for Traffic Safety notes, "Obscene gestures have gotten people shot, stabbed or beaten in every state." Remember, too, that the gesture need not be obscene to elicit a hostile response from another driver.

Use Your Horn and Lights Sparingly

As a rule, we should reserve horns and lights for warning other motorists of imminent danger. Don't use the horn to greet friends beside the road. Another driver might misinterpret your action. Apply the same rules to flashing your headlights. If you want to get another driver's attention for reasons other than an emergency, a short tap of the horn or a single flash of the lights is all you need.

Dim High Beams

Switch to low-beam headlights when you see another motorist either in front of you, going in your direction or coming toward you. When someone from behind passes you, dim your high beams as the other driver pulls even with your car. If an approaching driver refuses or forgets to dim high beams, don't retaliate. Dim your own headlights and focus on the right shoulder.

Keep Lane Free for Right Turns on Red

While states often require motorists to keep right except to pass or turn left, occupying the far right lane at an intersection can cause trouble if you plan to go straight. If another lane farther to the left will let you go straight, then leave the right lane clear for people who want to turn right on red.

Let Drivers Merge

Adjust your speed or lane position whenever possible to let other motorists merge.

Leave the Highway Carefully

Don't cut in front of another vehicle and then slow to leave the highway. Instead, pull in behind the vehicle. Also, don't pass a car within a half-mile of your exit unless that vehicle is traveling very slowly.

Don't Impede Traffic

If your vehicle can't keep up with the flow of traffic, pull over when it is safe to do so and let other drivers pass. Drivers of campers and trailers in mountainous areas should check their mirrors often to make sure they aren't becoming a rolling roadblock.

Avoid Eye Contact

While it generally is advisable to make eye contact with other drivers at intersections so you can be sure you are seen, it's not a good idea to lock eyes with a hostile motorist. This may incite a person with a volatile temper.

Exercise Your First-Amendment Rights Carefully

Many strongly worded bumper stickers and some symbols are sure to incite another driver somewhere. Think carefully before adding these to your car.

Maintain Car Alarms

Make sure your alarm system works properly and that you know how to turn it off quickly if it's triggered.

Don't Let Car Accessories Distract You

Distracted drivers who pay too little attention to traffic trigger many road-rage incidents.

Stay Out of Other Drivers' Blind Spots

Don't hang out in another driver's blind spot. Similarly, alter your speed to prevent other drivers from remaining in yours. If you don't, you might forget that the other motorist is there when you turn or change lanes. By the same token, don't position your car to block another motorist.

Allow Passing Drivers to Pass

If a driver wants to pass you, let him. Speeding up is sure to provoke anger.

Don't Pass and Then Slow Down

After passing another motorist, don't pull in front of the driver and then slow down, forcing him to pass you. If you pass, make sure you're going fast enough to avoid a potential conflict down the road.

If you're ever in a dispute with a driver who refuses to back off — even when you don't respond to provocations — never stop to discuss the matter, even if signaled to pull over. Keep driving. If the other driver follows you, don't go home or to your workplace. Instead, drive to a public, crowded area or, better yet, to a police station. If you have a cellular telephone and feel threatened, don't hesitate to call authorities.

Perhaps the old grade-school evaluation "plays well with others" shouldn't be retired after the fourth grade. In many ways, your ability and willingness to cooperate on the road — in essence, playing well with others — do more than make driving pleasant for all. They also contribute to your driving survival.

CHAPTER 7

Teenage Drivers

In This Chapter

• • • • • • • • • • •

- Why you need to consider your teen's maturity before beginning driver training

- Assessing training programs

- What driver's training can and can't do

- How you have been training your teen for years

- What to look for in a teen's first car

The thought of training a teen to drive strikes fear in the hearts of most parents, as well it should. Teenage drivers have a poor track record. During their first year of driving, they're twice as likely as the average adult driver to have an accident or be ticketed for a major infraction. They often drive as though they're invincible. As the statistics show, they aren't.

> **DID YOU KNOW?**
>
> Statistics that track motor-vehicle deaths by age provide much evidence of teenage immaturity, lack of driving experience and risk-taking behavior. Each year, 30 of every 100,000 16- to 19-year-olds die in motor-vehicle crashes. That compares to 13 of every 100,000 people in the 50- to 54-year age group and 28 of every 100,000 80- to 84-year-olds.

Most problems that plague teen drivers can be attributed to their age, lack of experience and lack of development. Despite what they think, they're not adults. They're still maturing, physically and mentally. They can be awkward and clumsy. Often they lack the maturity and judgment to handle driving and complex traffic situations.

Society has set 16 as the appropriate age to begin driving. As in all age-related issues, the rule may make sense for the population as a whole, but not for every individual. No doubt some 14-year-olds could handle the physical demands of controlling a vehicle and have the maturity to drive safely. Some 18-year-olds have neither capability but still carry a license.

Don't Let Teens Start Too Soon

Teens shouldn't drive until they are ready. Teens — and adults, for that matter — who wish to drive must clear three hurdles before they start training.

- Potential drivers must be able to control a vehicle. They must have sufficient size and strength to operate the controls, good vision, good reflexes, good coordination and the ability to process information quickly, weigh risks and draw appropriate, split-second conclusions.

- They must be able and willing to learn. Before driving, they must memorize traffic laws and be able to apply their knowledge while operating a car. In addition, they need to learn how a vehicle's controls work so they can operate them easily.

DID YOU KNOW?

An example of a parent who shouldn't have let his son proceed with driving lessons is the dad who went out of his way to deliver a check to the driving school before the behind-the-wheel lessons started.

"You didn't need to do that," the school administrator said. "Your son could have given the check to the instructor."

"I couldn't trust my son with that check," the father responded.

- They must be emotionally mature. They should handle setbacks well while remaining cooperative in their dealings with others. They should recognize that becoming a better driver is a process that demands continuing effort over a lifetime.

Parents with a teenager who behaves poorly shouldn't assume that the child's conduct will improve when he or she starts driving. Such cases are probably a happy coincidence, a byproduct of each day adding to the teen's maturity. More often than not, granting irresponsible teens the privilege to drive won't make them any more capable. If you can't trust your child, it's best to wait before beginning driver training. This isn't a punishment, although your teen may interpret it as such. Rather, the delay gives your teen more time to mature and develop. You don't do your children — or society — any favor by letting them drive too soon.

Practice, Practice, Practice

Whether you decide to train your teen to drive yourself, enroll him or her in a high school program or go to a commercial driving school, you or another responsible adult must be involved in the process. No beginner can learn to drive adequately in the few hours of behind-the-wheel training most professional or school-run programs provide.

Parents Play a Key Role

Even parents who enroll their teenagers in high school programs or professional training schools must be involved. Practice is crucial for enabling a teenager to drive adequately.

You have to take your child out for a great deal of real-world practice. *AAA's Teaching Your Teen to Drive*, a parent/teen novice-driving program available on CD-ROM and videotape, provides helpful advice; to order, call 800/327-3444.

This doesn't mean you should reject a school program or professional training. Most training programs include classroom lessons about traffic laws and vehicle operation, while professional behind-the-wheel training acquaints your teen with the right way to leave and enter traffic, select lanes, merge, make turns, deal with simple and complex traffic patterns and execute other safe driving maneuvers.

Just as a football coach or music teacher can instill valuable techniques, so, too, can a professional driving instructor help teens make faster progress while ensuring that they don't pick up bad habits.

Not all professional training schools or instructors are equal. Always evaluate the quality of the program. Here are factors you should consider.

- **Is the school licensed and insured?** Ask to see the appropriate certificates for both the school and the instructors. Then check with your state's licensing bureau and the insurance commissioner to verify what you were shown.

- **Who will instruct?** While the school's owner or director may have impressive qualifications, the training and experience of the people who teach your child in the classroom and behind the wheel should be your biggest concern. What certificates do they hold? How long have they been teaching? When did they last attend training to keep their knowledge up to date? Where did they go for that training?

- **How big are classes?** While state regulations differ, classes larger than 20 or 25 often mean less individual attention.

- **What textbook is used, and when was it last revised?** Look through it. If the school doesn't use a textbook, keep looking for one that does.

- **Is the classroom curriculum presented in sequence,** or may students drop into classes when time permits and in any order? To be more accessible to busy teens, many driving schools let students take classes in any order. Your child might be trained on highway driving before learning basic maneuvers in the classroom. Other schools require students to take classes in a specific order — rather like teaching addition and subtraction before going on to multiplication and division.

- **What audio-visual materials are used?** Some schools rely heavily on videos. Others don't. Ask how old the videos are. While older tapes may present valid information, the cars, fashions and hairstyles can easily distract teenagers.

- **Is the classroom pleasant and well maintained?** Is it conducive to learning? Is the school in a safe area? If classes are at night, what happens if you're late picking up your child?

- **How does the behind-the-wheel training work?** In some schools, students are trained one-on-one. In others, several teens go out together and take turns driving with the instructor. Still other school systems allow several students, each in a separate car, to go out together in a large, closed parking lot to practice maneuvers while an instructor oversees the session. How are the cars equipped? How well are they maintained?

- **Does the behind-the-wheel training cover all aspects of driving?** Some programs, for example, don't take students on limited-access highways.

- **What emergency maneuvers are taught?** How your child handles emergencies could mean the difference between life and death.

- **What assistance does the school provide when it's time to take the test for a license?** Some schools provide the car and even a testing site. Others don't. If the school furnishes any of these services, is there an extra charge?

- **What is the school's success rate?** What percentage of students pass the driving test the first time?

- **Finally, ask to sit in on a class before deciding.** Don't judge a school by the price of the program.

Although your teen has watched you drive for years, don't assume that he or she has a great deal of knowledge on the subject. Many children don't pay sufficient attention to realize what their parents are doing or why. For example, the number of beginning students who can't turn on the headlights or the defroster is staggering, even though most teens have seen their parents do it hundreds of times.

While children don't always pick up driving basics from their parents, they often adopt their parents' bad habits. If you roll through stop signs, consistently drive over the speed limit or cut off other motorists, don't be surprised if your beginning driver does these things, too.

Prepare for Challenges

Whether you do all the training or provide practice opportunities to complement a professional program, you can be sure to face challenges.

Awkward Operation

Behind-the-wheel beginners are clumsy. They often apply either too little or too much pressure on the gas or the brake and turn the steering wheel excessively or not enough.

Confusion About Controls

Many new drivers make significant mistakes. It's not unusual for a novice to mistake the gas and brake pedals. They forget to shift from drive to reverse, or vice versa, and then are surprised when they go in the wrong direction. They may steer too much going into corners and then fail to return the wheel to its straight-ahead position.

Lack of Practical Application

While new drivers may know the laws governing vehicle operation, they may not be able to apply them to actual situations the first few times without help.

Lagging Mental Stamina

Students may not be able to concentrate on driving for more than 30 minutes when they first start.

Take It One Step at a Time

Pick a safe place — an empty parking lot is good — for the first session. Let your teen get the feel of the car and its controls. Only after your aspiring driver is comfortable in this environment should you progress to relatively straight, wide streets with little traffic, slow speed limits and gentle curves.

While in the parking lot, practice taking control of the car from the passenger's seat if your teen makes a mistake. This may require you to steer, which power assist should make possible even from the passenger seat. To slow a car with an automatic transmission, shift to neutral. You also can turn off the ignition key in a real emergency, although this will instantly cut power steering. If your car has a center handbrake lever, apply the parking brake after shifting to neutral and keep your thumb on the release so you can control the level of braking. The parking brake won't stop your car as quickly as the foot brake, but it will slow the car and eventually stop it in an emergency. Make sure this brake is properly adjusted before starting to teach your teen to drive.

Talk your teen through new maneuvers before he or she performs them. Demonstrate first, then let the teen try it. Explain what happens and what should be done as you approach turns and intersections.

Communicate clearly. Reserve "right" for the direction and use "correct" to confirm an action.

SAFETY It's easy to shift a vehicle with an automatic transmission into neutral — but it's also easy to inadvertently shift into reverse. While many cars won't actually try to move backward in such circumstances, others will. Also, you definitely don't want to engage park while the car is moving. To avoid shifting into reverse or park on a car with a column-mounted shift lever, push the lever forward, toward the instrument panel, as you move it from drive to neutral. In most cars, this prevents engaging reverse or park. Most automatic transmission cars with a floor shift can be shifted only as far as neutral if the release button is not pushed in. Learn how your vehicle works before you start lessons.

Don't yell. Raising the emotional temperature inside the car can damage the learning process.

Beginning drivers who have ridden a bicycle, driven go-carts or used a lawn tractor often do better than those who haven't had these experiences. In addition, students who participate in sports or play musical instruments often demonstrate better physical coordination and process what they see on the road more quickly so they can take appropriate action.

Don't be satisfied when your child does a maneuver correctly once or twice. The practice is adequate only when your child can perform the maneuver correctly every time, even when given little time to prepare for it mentally.

Spend at least 50 hours, preferably 100 hours or more, driving with your teen before he or she goes for the state driving test. Most school programs offer only six hours of in-car instruction along with 30 hours of classes.

Once teens are licensed, parents have to stay involved to ensure their safety. A beginning driver isn't qualified to face all traffic and weather conditions at any hour of the day or night. During the first year, let your licensed teen drive only in areas and at times that match his or her skills. As ability improves, let the teen tackle more complex traffic patterns and go farther from home.

Before letting your teen go solo to the next step in traffic speed or complexity, accompany him or her on a practice trip to an area with comparable conditions. This will let you see whether the teen has made as much progress as you think. It's not unusual for a new driver who becomes exceptionally competent in a familiar suburban environment to make major errors in heavy traffic and when driving at freeway speeds.

DID YOU KNOW?

A surprising number of teens think that when the state grants them a license, it's proof that they're qualified to drive anywhere, under any circumstances. This is simply not true. Convincing many new drivers of this is a battle that you, as the parent, can't afford to lose.

Just as toddlers often want to run before they can walk, your newly licensed driver probably wants to rush through the steps of driver development. Don't let that happen. Just as with any activity, your child's driving will improve with practice and experience. Not only that, but as time passes he or she should mature, too.

Pick the Right Vehicle

A licensed teen's first request is usually to have his or her own car. To limit your teen's driving in the beginning, say no. Instead, let the teen use the family vehicle under appropriate guidelines. Your teen will be safer.

Some circumstances, however, may make the no-car rule impractical. Maybe you live far from public transportation and carpool routes, or your teen needs to attend classes, lessons or sporting events at times when no family member or friend can offer a lift. In such cases you may have to let your teen get a car. Nonetheless, it is wise to couple this privilege with performance standards, such as maintaining a high grade-point average, completing chores at home and avoiding crashes and tickets.

Selecting the right car is important. Seven guidelines can help you do this.

- The car should handle safely, especially in an emergency. This doesn't mean your teen should have a sports car — just the opposite. The lightning-fast response times and ample power that make a sports car a joy for an experienced driver are just what a teen doesn't need. Seek out a car that's stable when going straight, yet easy to control during an emergency lane change or mid-corner braking.

- The vehicle should have a low center of gravity to help your teen avoid rolling over in a skid or crash.

- Antilock brakes and, if you can find it, traction control are desirable features.

- The car should offer good crash protection to passengers. These days, fortunately, even older models are likely to have air bags. Other desirable safety devices include height-adjustable shoulder belts, rear-seat shoulder belts (rather than lap belts with no shoulder harnesses) and head restraints that can be adjusted and then locked in place.

- Even though rear-seat shoulder belts are recommended, rear-seat passengers are not. Parents shouldn't allow multiple passengers in the car during a teen's first year behind the wheel, even if the state doesn't spell out the restriction as part of a graduated licensing program.

- While the car should be large enough to protect occupants in a crash, it should also be small enough to maneuver easily. Although rarely a teen's first choice, midsize sedans can be perfect.

- The car shouldn't be too powerful. Buying your teen a high-performance car or truck shows poor judgment — on your part.

Limit Your Teen's Passengers

Passengers can distract teenage drivers from the task at hand. It is recommended that teenagers transport no passengers in their first year of driving and thereafter no more than one — and always in the front seat.

- The car should be reliable. Teens can easily become victims when a car breaks down. Reliability requires good maintenance.

There often is a final overriding requirement for a teenager's car: It has to be cheap. Fortunately, there are reasonably priced cars that meet all of these requirements. Unfortunately, few are at the top of a typical teen's list of "cool" vehicles.

> **DID YOU KNOW?**
>
> To help teenagers survive their first year of driving, AAA clubs across the country worked with state legislators to adopt graduated driver licensing. A complete program consists of four parts.
>
> 1. Beginning drivers go through a learner's permit period before they can be tested for a driver's license. During this time, they can drive only with a licensed adult.
>
> 2. For six to 12 months, newly licensed drivers can't carry more than one teenage passenger.
>
> 3. During this same time, new drivers can't drive late at night.
>
> 4. A ticket during this time means automatic enrollment in a retraining program. While most states have adopted at least some aspects of graduated driver licensing — and initial statistical analyses suggest that it really works — parents are urged to impose the full program on their teens.

Poor Choices

Domestic muscle cars from the late '60s and early '70s are popular with teens in some areas. They're relatively inexpensive and large enough to suggest a safety advantage in a collision with another vehicle. However, most also handle poorly, lack current safety technology and have too much power. Add poor fuel economy, aging components and, in some cases, older approaches to body design that may compromise safety in a crash, and the cars become a poor choice for novice drivers. Reject them for your teen.

A grandparent's 20-year-old sedan probably won't have air bags or antilock brakes. Choose something newer.

A convertible's canvas top offers no rollover protection, and most convertible bodies are structurally weaker than comparable coupes from the same manufacturer.

Also reject cars from the late '80s and early to mid-'90s with automatic seat belts. Some systems have a motorized shoulder belt and a manual lap belt that's fastened separately. Forgetting to use the lap belt makes this system dangerous. Seat belts mounted to the front door, rather than the pillar between the front and rear doors, also are undesirable. If a crash opens the door, the belt offers little protection.

Compact sport-utility vehicles and pickups may have an undesirably high center of gravity, sluggish handling and poor brakes. Some teens also may be tempted to carry friends in the open bed of a pickup.

High-powered vehicles — toys for adults — are always inappropriate for teens.

Draw Up Contracts

Many parents find it useful to write down the rules a teen is expected to follow once he or she has a license and access to a car. Rules can be negotiated, and the responsibilities of both the teen and the parents should be spelled out.

Breaking any rule must result in an appropriate punishment. For example, evidence of drinking or unsafe operation should mean suspension of all driving privileges for at least a year, even if no crash or police action resulted.

A father who saw his 17-year-old son deliberately spin the tires on one of the family's cars when leaving a drive-in restaurant took drastic action. He physically took the teen's license and suspended his right to drive any family vehicle until he reached age 21. He stuck to his decision as he put his son through college. Incidentally, the teen's younger siblings established excellent driving records when it came their turn to get a license.

Parents should also keep a close eye on the vehicle.

To make the agreement official, parents and the teen should sign it. Then, to keep it meaningful, they must live up to it. Here are sample contracts you may choose to use.

SAMPLE CONTRACT BETWEEN PARENTS AND TEEN

TEEN'S AGREEMENTS

- I will obey driving laws and operate motor vehicles safely.

- I will always wear a seat belt and make my passengers do the same.

- I will maintain my grades, conduct and attitude at the same high level as when I was granted driving privileges.

- I won't allow anyone else to drive a vehicle entrusted to me.

- I won't drink and drive or ride with anyone who has been drinking or who may drive recklessly. I'll call you for a ride if I think I'll have a problem arriving home safely. If I can't reach you, I'll call for a taxi. You'll pay for it, and I won't be punished.

- I'll transport no teenage passengers during my first year driving. After the first year, I will carry no more than one and only in the front seat. I'll never transport passengers in the back seat.

- During my first year of driving, I won't eat, drink or use a cell phone while driving.

- I'll be home by _____ o'clock on weekends and _____ o'clock on weeknights.

- I won't take any long trips for any reason.

- I'll contribute $_____ toward insurance, maintenance and other driving expenses.

- I'll perform the following chores

_____

_____

_____

Being issued a ticket or warning or failing to obey the above rules may result in my driving privilege being revoked.

_____

Signature   Date

SAMPLE CONTRACT BETWEEN PARENTS AND TEEN
PARENT'S AGREEMENTS

- When riding in a vehicle, I promise to always wear my seat belt.

- I'll never drive when I've been drinking.

- I will answer your questions about drugs and alcohol calmly, openly and honestly.

- I will provide or arrange for safe transportation anytime, under any circumstances when you ask for it. In dealing with such a situation, I will remain calm and discuss it with you only when we both can communicate in a calm and sober manner.

- I will contribute $_____ toward insurance, maintenance and other driving expenses.

_____

Signature   Date

CHAPTER 8

Older Drivers

In This Chapter

• • • • • • • • • • • •

- How growing older can affect your driving

- What medical problems have the greatest effect on driving

- How older drivers can reduce risk

- Some traffic situations to avoid

Aging, the classic one-liner goes, isn't so bad when you consider the alternative.

Growing older does bring new challenges. Tasks that used to be easy — including driving — can take more time and effort and, in some cases, become completely impossible.

Older drivers face a trade-off. Although hearing, vision and reflexes may not be as acute as a teenager's, years of accumulated experience can give mature drivers superior judgment that helps make up for such shortfalls. Older drivers often know what they can and can't do and choose ways to avoid difficult situations.

It's impossible to make a blanket statement about when someone should quit driving. Just as teens mature at their own pace, so do elders experience aging on their own timetable. One 80-year-old may be perfectly capable of driving safely while a 65-year-old is a regular terror on the road.

You might not even realize when you can no longer drive safely. Your abilities may decline so gradually that neither you nor your loved ones recognize that you no longer have the skills to avoid a serious crash.

When comparing crash death rates per miles driven, drivers older than 74 are second only to inexperienced teens and drivers in their early 20s. Yet the Insurance Institute for Highway Safety suggests this may not be a fair indictment of older motorists' driving skills. The number may, instead, reflect that older, more fragile bodies are less likely to withstand the trauma inflicted in a crash. Crashes from which teens would walk away can be far more serious — even fatal — for their grandparents.

Watch for Early Signs

Here are some early signs of diminished ability to look for in yourself or your loved ones.

Medical Problems Take a Toll

Most people believe deteriorating vision and dementia are an older driver's major problems, but a growing body of evidence suggests that far more common diseases take a bigger toll on driving ability.

Motorists with heart conditions, circulatory problems, diabetes, hearing loss or slowing reflexes crash more often than people without these problems. Arthritis, loss of muscle tone and difficulty controlling the hands or feet also can affect driving safety. If you suffer from a growing number of medical problems, talk about driving with all of the doctors involved in your care.

If you take prescriptions or over-the-counter medications, ask your doctors and pharmacists how the drugs could affect your driving. If you have multiple prescriptions from more than one doctor, make sure all of the physicians and pharmacists involved know about all of the medications. One drug by itself might not affect your driving, but in combination with others, it could have serious safety consequences.

Medical problems also should prompt you to seek out a professionally administered driving evaluation. Such sessions are designed to test your skills in a variety of driving situations and can last an hour or more. This will often require an hour or more on the road so that the session can include all the traffic situations and types of roads you normally encounter.

Evaluations are available from many sources, including some private and governmental agencies. Driving schools in your area also may offer the service. Evaluators should have experience dealing with drivers with your specific medical condition. Even if they don't, however, their observations can be valuable. Be sure to ask for a written report afterward.

Your Passengers Are Jittery

Don't dismiss fidgety riders. Making your passengers nervous could be a sign that you're doing something wrong behind the wheel. Some older drivers would rather believe their peers have become more anxious with age than acknowledge that their own capabilities have deteriorated.

Dents and Dings Mar Your Car

If you've begun to inflict a number of minor scrapes and dings on your car, your driving skills may have slipped. Even if your car remains dent-free, frequent run-ins with curbs and other objects once easily avoided should alert you to a problem.

Traffic Is so Confusing

When you're behind the wheel, you have more to do than just point the car in a straight line. You have to watch other cars around you, ahead of you and behind you. You must be aware of pedestrians, and adjust the radio or air conditioner. You have to change lanes so you can turn left at the next intersection. Older drivers sometimes have difficulty processing all the information they collect in time to act appropriately. If you worry about merging into traffic, find intersections increasingly difficult or have a hard time keeping track of vehicles around you, your driving ability may be declining.

SAFETY

As a driving evaluator, I often must deliver bad news. One elderly woman whose driving seriously concerned her family members consented to an evaluation. At the end of the session, she didn't realize she had arrived at her home of more than 30 years. The recommendation to discontinue driving was obvious, but she found it hard to accept nonetheless.

You're Lost on Familiar Streets

If you occasionally have trouble knowing where you are when driving on familiar streets, seek medical advice. Stop driving until you receive a clean bill of health.

You Make Mistakes with Controls

Choosing the wrong gear or the wrong pedal can have life-threatening implications. If you or loved ones notice this problem, a medical review is in order.

Those Speed Limits Are Too High

Many drivers speed. Others are uncomfortable driving at the posted limit, even under ideal conditions. If you frequently travel 5, 10 or even 20 mph under the speed limit — even in good weather and light traffic — you could have a problem. Seek medical advice and a driving evaluation.

PITFALLS Sometimes people can be overly critical of an older person's driving and mistake reasonable caution for indecision. At a commercial driving school, I evaluated a woman whose family members derided her for her lack of speed. The conclusion: She was aware of surrounding traffic, coped well with complex situations and showed good judgment at intersections, often a critical area for older drivers.

It's Hard to See at Night

Many drivers, even younger ones, have trouble seeing adequately at night. Good daytime vision is no guarantee that you can see well after dark. Nighttime driving requires the ability to see in low-light conditions and recover quickly from glare. Problems with either should prompt a thorough eye examination. Also, have your eyes checked if you notice flares or rings around bright light sources at night.

Driving in the Dark

WONDERFILE.COM

If driving at night intimidates you, regardless of your age, you're wise to restrict your driving to daylight hours.

Police Pull You Over

Most traffic stops start when a police officer notices something disturbing in a person's driving — even if the driver doesn't get a ticket. If you've recently gotten a ticket, a warning or simply a little friendly advice from an officer, you may want to have your driving skills evaluated.

Oops! You Crashed

Forget legal responsibility. Even if you weren't at fault, you should think seriously about what you did or didn't do that contributed to your recent crash. A number of techniques can significantly reduce the likelihood of crashing. Maybe it's time for you to attend a driver improvement program designed to help experienced motorists hone their skills.

> **DID YOU KNOW?** Deteriorating driving abilities often necessitate a major life change. During an evaluation, an older woman whose abilities were significantly impaired told me that she desperately needed to keep her license. She lived in the country with no nearby family and could no longer burden friends for rides to the store, the doctor or church services. After I found her incapable of continuing to drive, I suggested she move closer to mass transit and the support services that would make it possible for her to continue to live independently. Plan for the possibility that you'll have to stop driving by making wise choices about where and how you will live.

Many older drivers know instinctively that they aren't as sharp as they once were. In some cases, they compensate by changing driving patterns. Those who can't see well after dark quit driving at night, for instance. Drivers who have trouble in heavy traffic shift their trips to non-peak travel times. Those intimidated by freeway speeds and traffic stay away from limited-access highways, particularly during peak periods.

Choose Intersections Wisely

Proper route planning can help you avoid some risky maneuvers. Intersections with lights or all-way stop signs are safer than intersections with just a simple two-way stop or a yield sign because they control the flow of traffic better. Drivers who worry about their ability to handle a crossroads can greatly reduce collision danger by choosing the safer intersection.

Your best option is an intersection with lights that feature left- or right-turn arrows. The signals help you turn safely by stopping all other traffic. But be alert: Though signals greatly reduce the likelihood of a problem, not all drivers obey their signal. Use caution before proceeding through any intersection.

Left turns in the face of oncoming traffic are particularly difficult, especially for older drivers. If turning under the protection of a left-turn arrow isn't an option, you sometimes can avoid a left turn by making three right turns instead. Go straight past your left turn, and then drive around the block by turning right three times.

Not all drivers whose skills are declining are willing to admit or even recognize their behind-the-wheel shortcomings. For these motorists, states may require a limited or graduated license. It can limit vehicle operation to daylight hours, preclude freeway driving or require the driver to use a vehicle outfitted with special equipment.

Just as commercial pilots brush up on flying skills and office workers are sent for training on new equipment, drivers should renew their skills and knowledge regularly through additional training, such as programs developed by AAA. The courses review recent changes in automotive technology, traffic patterns and motor-vehicle laws so experienced drivers can bring their knowledge up to date. As an added inducement, many insurance companies offer discounts to policyholders who complete such a course. Call your local AAA office for details on programs in your area.

If Necessary, Get Retested

Retesting all drivers regularly, both on the road and in a written exam covering traffic laws, is one way to identify motorists whose skills are deficient, regardless of age. That it isn't done reflects the unpopular nature of retesting.

Even a vision screening before license renewal has proven difficult to implement in many states. Most states require insurance companies to offer reduced rates to older drivers who enroll in certain driver-improvement courses. Many states also have programs to retest drivers whose abilities seem to have slipped. Often, the observation of a police officer or recommendation of a family member or a physician prompts the retest.

If you believe a member of your family needs to be retested, you'll do this person and society no favor by ignoring the problem. Contact your local driver's license bureau to learn the process in your state.

The number of older Americans will swell drastically between 2010 and 2030 when baby boomers start reaching age 65, according to the Administration on Aging. This increasing number of older people, many of whom will continue driving for as long as they can, already has prompted automobile manufacturers to redesign some vehicles and their safety systems. If these trends continue, look for larger, less-confusing controls and a wider application of the newest safety systems, including "smart" air bags that determine where and how far from the air bag a passenger is seated before "deciding" how quickly to inflate in a crash. More and more vehicles also will be equipped with side air bags and side-curtain air bags. Seat belt pretensioners combined with force limiters also will benefit older and younger passengers.

The growing population of older citizens also should prompt supplemental transportation programs for people who can't drive. Such programs, which often fill gaps in public transportation, may serve only seniors or include the disabled and other specific groups who can't or don't drive. Funded by government, nonprofit organizations, church groups and businesses, the systems provide door-to-door transportation in most cases for medical appointments, shopping, social gatherings or religious services. Even many rural areas offer supplemental services, which can give people transportation and a sense of independence. For options in your area, check with local governmental and social service agencies.

CHAPTER 9

Maintaining a Vehicle

In This Chapter

• • • • • • • • • • • •

- Why routine maintenance is important

- Why the maintenance schedule you've been following may be wrong

- What instruments and warning lights really tell you

- How to find a service facility

How well you maintain your vehicle directly affects your driving safety. A well-maintained car will be dependable and will handle responsively. A poorly maintained car is much more likely to break down and be difficult to control, especially in an emergency. The formula is simple: Good maintenance plus prompt repairs equals greater safety for you and your family.

Unfortunately, many people ignore basic maintenance. In today's vehicles, the effects of neglect can take years to become apparent. Once a problem caused by poor maintenance does arise, the consequences may be significant and costly.

Lucky for you, basic vehicle maintenance is simple. First, read the owner's manual. It contains a wealth of information, including explanations of how to operate the vehicle's systems and accessories and an outline of the maintenance needed to keep the vehicle running smoothly.

Keep Up with Maintenance

Manufacturers take two approaches to owner's manuals and maintenance schedules. Some list the maintenance requirements in the manual; others include a separate maintenance book. Unfortunately, some dealers substitute their own official-looking maintenance book — which may call for more maintenance than necessary or even leave out important steps — for the factory-supplied one. It's best to use the manufacturer's maintenance book.

If you were given a substitute, ask the dealer for the factory-supplied maintenance manual. If it is unavailable, call the toll-free number in the back of the owner's manual to request one from the automaker.

> **PITFALLS**
>
> Though they don't do it often, automakers have been known to change their minds about what constitutes proper mainte- nance after problem reports start coming in from owners. The manu- facturers then issue bulletins to dealers on revised maintenance requirements, as well as procedures for eliminating a problem. In addition, climate and your individual driving habits may make it important to perform some services more often than outlined in the owner's manual. If a dealer recommends more service than what's specified in the factory maintenance schedule, ask why. The reason should be compelling, and if it's based on a factory bulletin, ask to review a copy of it.

In most cases, manufacturers recommend performing maintenance on mileage or time intervals. Oil changes — which some manufacturers recommend every 3,000 miles or 90 days, whichever comes first — are a good example. Drivers who cover an average of 12,000 miles annually can expect to cover 3,000 miles every 90 days, making the recommendation for mileage and time one and the same.

What if you drive more or less than that? If you drive 36,000 miles a year, the 3,000-mile interval will mean changing the oil monthly. If you drive 6,000 miles a year, you still must change the oil every 90 days, even though you're only changing it at 1,500-mile intervals.

> **DID YOU KNOW?**
>
> Despite the complexity of today's cars, many owners — and maybe you, too — still do their own oil changes. This is fine as long as you realize that an oil change involves more than just changing the oil and filter. It also should include a complete look under the hood and under the body of the car. You or a technician should look for leaks and damaged or broken components in the suspension, exhaust, brake and fuel systems; check all fluid levels; and examine the condition of belts, hoses and battery connections. Any problems can be addressed before they become serious or do expensive damage. Also, follow proper procedures when disposing of used fluids.

Many maintenance procedures fall under the time or mileage formula. Including time as a service trigger acknowledges that cars deteriorate even when they aren't driven. Coolant, drive belts, hoses and other parts need to be changed regularly, even if the car has accumulated only a few miles since the service was last performed.

Time and mileage intervals also vary based on two common service schedules: one for normal and another for severe usage. Which usage pattern is right for you? Your owner's manual should tell you.

Most people are shocked to discover that the manufacturer characterizes their driving style as "severe." Short trips, stop-and-go driving, prolonged idling, driving in extremely hot or cold temperatures, driving in dusty conditions either through construction zones or on dirt roads, towing a trailer, navigating wet or snowy roads or driving at high altitudes may qualify as severe usage. If you meet just one criterion, your usage is severe.

Take an Active Role in Car Care

While most people turn maintenance over to a professional at a dealership or independent garage, drivers can and should handle many checkups themselves on a regular basis.

Check at Each Refueling

Each time you refuel, check the engine oil and examine the belts and hoses under the hood. Also look at the coolant overflow tank. Don't remove caps while the engine is hot without first reviewing the proper procedure in your owner's manual. In most cases, you should be able to see the coolant level in the reservoir without having to remove the cap. On many cars you also can see the level of brake fluid through the translucent reservoir. Finally, check the windshield washer reservoir. The owner's manual will outline any other checks to complete at this time.

Check Some Items Monthly

At least once a month, check tire pressures when the car is cold. Driving to a filling station, even if the distance is short, can heat the tires enough through sidewall flexing to affect the reading. During warm weather, the only way to get an accurate reading is to check when the vehicle has been left unused for at least four hours. No glove compartment should be without a quality tire-pressure gauge. As for the spare, it needs checking at least every three months. Always use the same gauge, and don't trust a gauge attached to an air hose.

Keep Tires Inflated

Check the pressure in each of your vehicle's tires monthly.

Check the operation of all the lights at least monthly. This is an easy one: When you pull into a garage, carport or parking space at night, look against the wall for distinct pockets of light from each headlight. Check high and low beams as well as fog lights, then turn the headlights and fog lights off and operate only the parking lights, which should cast an amber glow against the garage wall. Turn on the directional signals to make sure they flash. When stopped in traffic at night, you often can use reflections on the vehicle behind you to check the tail lights, brake lights and rear directional signals. In addition, walk around the car to be sure that the side marker and license plate lights are working properly. You might need help checking the backup lights.

At least once monthly, check the wiper blades, including the rear wiper system if your vehicle has one. If they are hardened or brittle rather than smooth, replace them at once. Also replace them if they are cracked or torn.

SAFETY While the owner's manual may not mention it, regular maintenance also includes cleaning the windows, mirrors and exterior lights. Wash both the outside and inside of windows, especially if your car is driven by a smoker or is often parked in the hot sun. Cleaning headlights also is important since dirt can block much of their light output.

Perform Other Routine Maintenance

In addition to these checks, automobile makers outline several more maintenance procedures. Follow the schedule for changing fuel and air filters, engine coolant and transmission fluid. Cars with a timing belt will need that part changed regularly.

> **DID YOU KNOW?**
>
> Changing a timing belt is expensive, but there's no good alternative. A broken belt will leave you stranded and may result in costly internal engine damage. If your engine uses the timing belt to drive the water pump, changing the water pump at the same time is a good idea. You also should have the camshaft, crankshaft and idler shaft oil seals checked. Finally, examine the timing belt tensioner and replace it if it's in poor condition.

The manufacturer also recommends regular inspections of the brakes, brake hoses, shocks/struts, exhaust system and fuel lines. Other items to inspect include seals and boots, drive-shaft bearings and joints and all fluid levels. Regular tire rotation and checks of the suspension system and alignment are on the list as well.

Modern ignition systems have become remarkably dependable. Advanced electronics have made it possible to replace the entire distributor — points, condenser, rotor, cap and wiring — with a computer that controls a coil pack that fires one or two spark plugs. A six-cylinder car has either three or six coils. In many models, platinum-tipped spark plugs won't need replacing until the vehicle has been driven 100,000 miles.

Manufacturers sometimes fail to recommend procedures that should be done, such as brake fluid changes. Since brake fluid absorbs water, often from humidity in the air, regular brake fluid changes make sense. Automakers who do recommend this step suggest doing it every two years or 24,000 miles. This is especially important on cars with antilock brakes since components can be exceptionally expensive to replace.

While repairs aren't considered maintenance, you're wise to take care of them as soon as you discover a problem. Immediate repairs will restore your car's dependability and make it safer. They also can save you money.

Sometimes a broken or worn component can damage other parts. For example, a broken shock absorber not only roughens the ride, but makes repairs to the tire and

DID YOU KNOW? Many maintenance procedures generate hazardous waste. If you work on your car yourself, contact the local environmental protection department for the proper procedures for disposing of used oil, oil filters, oil containers, antifreeze, brake fluid, batteries and tires. Some cleaners, polishes and automotive paints also can be hazardous if mishandled and may be a fire hazard if improperly stored.

the suspension system necessary as well. Delay fixing squealing brakes and, in addition to new pads, you might also need new rotors.

Interpret Gauges and Warning Lights

In addition to supplying an information-packed maintenance manual, automakers also inform you via gauges and warning lights on the instrument panel. Yet as useful as this information can be, many drivers don't know how to interpret some of the readings. You probably have a good grasp of what the speedometer and fuel gauge tell you, but it's a good idea to familiarize yourself with what the rest of the instruments do as well.

Understand the Instrument Panel

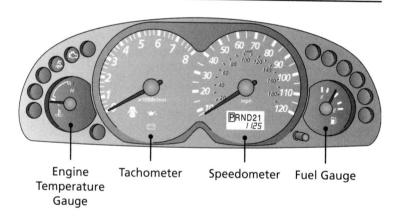

Engine Temperature Gauge   Tachometer   Speedometer   Fuel Gauge

Knowing what your vehicle's gauges and warning lights are trying to tell you can enable you to pinpoint a potential problem quickly.

Keep an Eye on Engine Speed

The tachometer, or tach as it's often called, measures engine speed. An engine problem often shows up in a change in idle speed, so note this reading when the car is cold and again after it warms up. Investigate any change immediately. Many tachometers also have orange numbers on a short area around the rim, followed by a portion painted red. Generally, you can operate the engine in the orange zone for three or four seconds when you need maximum acceleration.

Never run the engine so the needle climbs over the "red line" into the red zone. In most cases, you can drive so your engine speed stays under 4,000 rpm — well below the red line.

High Temperature Can Damage the Engine

In most vehicles, the engine temperature gauge tells you the temperature of the engine's coolant. When you first start the engine after the car has sat unused for several hours, the needle should point toward "cold." After driving a while, it should move into the "normal" range. If it ever heads toward the "hot" end of the range, you have a problem that could result in extensive engine damage if you keep driving. If your engine overheats, jot down the conditions that prompted the gauge to climb too high. A technician can use your observations to diagnose the problem.

Some cars have a coolant temperature warning light instead of a gauge. A blue light usually comes on when the engine is cold. When the engine reaches normal operating temperature, the light goes out. If the engine becomes too hot, a red warning light comes on.

Unusual readings foreshadow many cooling system problems. Don't ignore them. Have a technician check out the cooling system immediately.

If you turn off a fully warmed vehicle for just a few minutes and then restart it, you may notice the temperature gauge peg to "hot" before returning to the normal range after 10 or 15 seconds of engine idling. This is probably normal.

Adequate Oil Pressure Can Protect the Engine

In vehicles with an oil-pressure gauge, the pressure should climb within seconds after you start a cold engine and the needle should jump to a relatively high reading. The pressure should gradually drop. After this point, higher readings indicate higher engine speeds.

A general rule calls for at least 10 pounds per square inch of oil pressure for every 1,000 rpm on the tachometer, although most car engines will develop twice this pressure on the road. If oil pressure drops too low, severe engine damage can happen in seconds. Don't drive any farther than necessary when the oil-pressure reading drops into the danger zone.

Some vehicles have an oil-pressure light that comes on if the pressure drops dangerously low. If you see the light while you're driving, stop as quickly as possible. A flickering oil light at idle may be a warning of serious troubles.

Neither a low reading on the gauge nor the sudden illumination of the light means that the oil level in the crankcase is low. While a low oil level can cause a low oil-pressure reading, an acceptable level of oil on the dipstick doesn't necessarily mean oil pressure is normal and the pressure gauge or warning light is wrong. You can have major, engine-destroying oil system problems even with ample oil in the crankcase.

Don't mistake an oil temperature gauge, offered on some cars, for an oil-pressure gauge. Its readings will be entirely different.

DID YOU KNOW? There are more sophisticated ways than watching the odometer or waiting for the warning light to come on to determine when an oil change is due. In newer vehicles, computers monitor engine usage, driving style and outside and engine temperatures to estimate when it's time to change the oil. If you drive the car harder or use it on short journeys in cold weather, expect the warning light to tell you to change the oil frequently. The computer lets you extend the interval if you take long, easy drives in moderate temperatures. Perhaps the best approach, taken by a few automakers, is a system that monitors the condition of oil in the crankcase.

High Voltage Can Hurt Electrical Systems

In cars with a voltmeter, expect readings of 14 to 15 volts most of the time. High readings of 17 or 18 volts for extended periods could mean the voltage regulator has failed. The resulting high voltage could damage the battery and some electrical devices.

A low reading means the alternator can't keep up with the electrical demand to run the engine and the vehicle's accessories. It could result from excessive demand for electrical power or a problem in the charging system. If low voltage is your only problem, you can usually drive for a short distance, depending on the charge in the battery when the problem began and the number of electrical accessories you use. The climate control system, rear defroster and headlights require significant amounts of current. To lengthen your driving range, turn off as many devices as possible.

A battery warning light usually indicates weak charging-system output. Treat it as you would a low voltage reading.

Pay Attention to Warning Lights

Warning lights, which usually are color-coded, let you determine the severity of a problem.

Green and blue lights — the ones that tell you the cruise control is engaged or the turn signals or high-beam headlights are on — are informational.

Amber or yellow lights that remain on — including the air bag light, "check engine soon" light and, in some cars, the antilock braking system light — warn of systems that should be checked quickly, within a day or two, but shouldn't leave you stranded.

Other systems also use a yellow warning light. When you activate traction control, a yellow light comes on to let you know that you're driving too aggressively for road conditions. When you back off the accelerator, the problem should disappear and the light will go out.

Red lights warn of the most serious problems. Ignore them — high engine temperature, low oil-pressure and brake-system lights, for instance — and you risk being stranded or having a significant mechanical failure.

AAA Inspects Service Facilities

It can be difficult to find a good service facility for regular maintenance or an emergency repair. Fortunately, AAA's Approved Auto Repair program takes much of the guesswork out of finding a good garage. Local AAA offices thoroughly check participating garages to ensure that they offer quality repair work. In addition, AAA members are entitled to a free safety inspection when paid maintenance or repair work is performed, a written estimate for all procedures, an extended warranty, the right to have most old parts returned and, in the unlikely event of a problem, dispute resolution through AAA. For all these reasons, it makes sense to look for the Approved Auto Repair sign on any service establishment you plan to use.

> **DID YOU KNOW?** Emission testing tells you more about your vehicle than the cleanliness of its exhaust. Cars that perform poorly often have something wrong with them that can affect dependability. Regard an emissions test as an opportunity to see how clean your vehicle is and how dependable it's likely to be. If a problem is found, have it fixed promptly — for your safety and the good of the environment.

Chapter 10

Handling Breakdowns

In This Chapter

• • • • • • • • • • • •

- How your car warns you before breaking down

- How to handle breakdowns

- What you should and should not fix yourself

- How to find service away from home

Although good maintenance can go a long way, it can't guarantee that your car will never break down. Breakdowns are rife with potential danger. They can leave you stranded far from civilization, sometimes at a late hour or during bad weather — or worse yet, hidden just over a hill or around a corner where approaching drivers have little time to react to your disabled vehicle. How you handle a breakdown can be critical to your survival.

Regular maintenance is the best way to avoid a breakdown. Although meticulous care can't guarantee you'll never have trouble, you'll likely have ample warning if things do go wrong. Some drivers ignore the warning signs. Some don't recognize them. Some, of course, have no warning at all.

Know Symptoms of Impending Breakdown

Because breakdowns can be dangerous, recognizing the symptoms is important. Here is what to look for:

Has Performance Changed?

A change in your vehicle's performance can let you know that trouble is coming. If you step on the gas and the vehicle stumbles and wheezes rather than moves ahead as it normally does, something is clearly wrong. Some problems may be intermittent, but don't expect them to cure themselves.

Is It Making Strange Noises?

Investigate a new or unusual noise immediately. A buzz that sounds like it's coming from the rear of your vehicle could be the first sign of a failing fuel pump. A whine when you corner could be a bad wheel bearing. Whatever the noise, check it out.

What's That Vibration?

A new vibration can be the first sign of trouble. Perhaps a tire is failing or an axle is coming apart. An engine could be misfiring or the transmission could be in the early stages of failure. Sudden roughness or vibration in a car that ran smoothly yesterday indicates an immediate need for service.

Is There a Leak?

A puddle under the car points to a problem that needs to be addressed immediately. With the possible exception of windshield washer fluid, every other liquid is vital to your car's proper operation. The sudden appearance of oil or coolant under your car means trouble. Get service at once.

One exception is water that the air conditioner spills on the ground. The liquid is the condensed humidity that the air conditioner extracted from the air while cooling it. Some systems discharge up to a pint of fluid while the car is parked. This is normal.

PITFALLS

Not all vehicle failures let you pull easily to the side of the road. For a *stuck throttle or sudden acceleration,* shift to neutral — even though doing so could cost you an engine — if you're unsure whether you can turn off the engine without also locking the steering wheel. If you turn off the engine, be prepared to exert far more force to steer and to press much harder on the brake pedal to stop the car. For *brake failure,* if pumping the brake two or three times quickly brings you to a stop, drive no farther and have the car towed. If pumping fails, use the parking brake. Apply the release mechanism at the same time to keep the wheels from locking. If this also fails, shift to a lower gear to slow down or turn off the engine. Practice in an empty parking lot. For a *tire blowout,* grip the steering wheel firmly to maintain control, but steer as little as possible. Gently let up on the accelerator to slow the car gradually. If needed, apply the brake gently. For *sudden headlight failure,* go from low beam to high beam, or vice versa. Try operating the light switch a few times. If your car has fog lights, turn them on. If nothing works, use the emergency flashers to guide you to a stop and get service before continuing to drive.

Are Fluids Disappearing without a Trace?

If fluids are low and you can't find a leak, check the situation quickly. Engine coolant, brake, transmission and power-steering fluids sometimes disappear without seeming to leave a trace. Despite the absence of puddles, such fluid loss is serious and needs to be investigated.

Are Instrument Readings Abnormal?

Unusual instrument readings alert you to potential trouble. Low voltage readings, unusual engine temperatures or any warning light that comes on tells you something is wrong.

Is Something Unusual Happening?

Unusual occurrences are signs of potentially bigger problems. A car suddenly emitting noticeable quantities of white, blue or black smoke has a definite problem. If the headlights suddenly dim when you come to a stop, check the battery or charging system.

All are warning signs of a pending failure, and each must be fixed. Doesn't it make sense to do the repairs before you get stuck in traffic? Fixing your car after you have it towed won't be any cheaper, and ignoring a problem could lead to additional costly damage. For the sake of your driving survival, have problems fixed as quickly as possible.

Vehicle Dies without Warning

What do you do if you have no warnings before the car leaves you stranded? The answer depends on how your car fails. If it just quits, then you're stuck where the car dies. But if your car sputters, almost dies, then runs roughly on the verge of quitting, or if you have a tire failure that still lets you drive slowly, follow these suggestions.

Look for Safe Place to Park

Find a spot where the shoulder is wide and visibility in all directions is good. If you can get the car off the road, either into a parking lot or by taking an exit ramp off a busy roadway, do so.

In the case of a flat tire, proceed to a safe place by driving slowly on the shoulder with your four-way flashers going, even if this ruins both the tire and the wheel. Choosing not to stop next to dangerous, high-speed traffic could be one of the wisest decisions you make, even if it does boost the cost of repairs — and if your car has alloy wheels, the cost of a replacement rim could be high.

Stop and take advantage of a good parking spot rather than risk the unknown around the corner or over the hill. Too many motorists refuse to believe a vehicle that suddenly begins to knock and smoke is about to die. They'll drive right by a perfect place to stop in hopes of making it to the next exit five miles away. Such a gamble can strand them in a place where approaching drivers have almost no warning that a disabled vehicle is ahead.

If a wide paved shoulder is waiting for you, be thankful. Park as far from the travel lane as you can. If there is no paved shoulder, pull off the highway onto dirt. If high grass or dried leaves are on the shoulder, be careful. They can come in contact with a hot catalytic converter and start a fire.

Keep in mind that a wide, highly visible parking spot on a left shoulder can be just as good as a spot on the right side of the road. If you are in the left lane when your car fails and you can't safely make it to the right shoulder, park in the best spot you can find on the left.

Warn Other Motorists

Turn on your four-way flashers, raise your hood and tie a white cloth to your door handle or antenna. Place flares or reflector triangles — which should be in your emergency kit — well behind your car to warn approaching drivers. Be extremely careful. Be sure you can walk safely — off the highway — to and from your car. On an interstate, the first warning device should be placed at least 300 feet behind your vehicle. Visualize the length of a football field or count off roughly 100 to 120 paces. At 60 mph, even this seemingly lengthy distance gives approaching drivers just three to four seconds of warning. Place the second device at about 100 feet and the third device about 10 feet behind your vehicle.

If you have no warning devices and your car is stranded where someone could crash into it, you need to warn approaching motorists. Stand about 300 feet back from your vehicle off to the side of the road and wave a white cloth such as a handkerchief; at night, use a flashlight. Do this only if you can walk easily and stand in a safe spot, preferably behind a roadside barrier.

> ## DID YOU KNOW?
>
> In deciding between flares or reflectors, consider these points. Nothing commands attention like a flare. Day or night, the bright light is a clear warning of trouble ahead. Unfortunately, flares burn for only 15 to 45 minutes. If you can't move your car or help doesn't arrive during that time, your flares will leave you unprotected as they die out. In addition, flares can be a fire hazard near dry grass or forests. Reflective triangles, though less compelling than flares, also attract attention, never burn out, can be used repeatedly and present no fire hazard. Most fold neatly into a small container that stores easily and have a weighted base to keep them from blowing over on windy days.

Stay out of Traffic

Don't walk in travel lanes, even if they appear to be temporarily clear. Never cross an expressway on foot.

Assess the Situation

If your car appears to be in a relatively safe position and is visible to oncoming traffic, stay inside it after setting out warnings. Lock your doors. If strangers stop to offer help, don't unlock your doors or go with them. Have them call police if you haven't already done so.

If your car is exposed to fast-moving traffic and in danger of being hit by an inattentive driver, get out of your car and wait in a safer spot. Leaving through the door away from traffic is usually safest.

Call for Help

Once you have warned other drivers and ensured your own safety, use your cellular telephone to call for help. If you don't have a cell phone or have broken down where you can't get a signal, wait for help.

On a CB radio, use channel 9, which is traditionally reserved for emergencies. Understand, however, that there is no guarantee that authorities will hear your call and a disreputable person won't.

If the highway has emergency roadside telephones every mile or so, walk to one — assuming you can do so safely, are in good physical condition and won't have to leave vulnerable passengers in the car. Keep track of where these phones are so you don't walk back nine-tenths of a mile when another is just one-tenth of a mile ahead.

SAFETY Emergency call center representatives often are frustrated when callers can't clearly explain where they have broken down. Make it a point to note mile-marker signs as you travel through unfamiliar territory, even if your car is running well, and know the direction in which you are traveling. Many telematics devices can pinpoint your position, often through the use of global positioning satellites, to within 50 feet to facilitate rescue efforts.

As unpleasant and potentially dangerous as a roadside breakdown is, following these steps should make the experience safer.

Do Your Own Repairs

At one time, a typical do-it-yourselfer could quickly analyze a problem under the hood and fix it with simple hand tools. Tales of repairs using nothing more than a paper clip, chewing gum and string have a romantic ring to them — and they once were possible. Determining what's wrong in today's vehicles, however, often requires an experienced technician armed with sophisticated electronic test equipment.

Still, some things you may be able to do for yourself.

Check the Gauges

You thought you filled the fuel tank yesterday, but did you? Also check for engine temperature and voltage if the instrument panel has these gauges. If the engine stalls, don't let warning lights mislead you. Nearly every light should come on if the engine is out of commission. Instead, note the warning lights that went on just before the engine died. If the car is completely dead, with no lights or gauge readings, the problem is electrical.

Check under the Hood

Turn off the ignition key and look under the hood. Something may be obviously wrong. Perhaps a wiring harness plug is disconnected or a plastic air passageway has ruptured. Reconnecting the plug or taping the air passage could get you to a garage for service.

If your car dies after hitting a rough stretch of pavement, check the electric fuel pump reset, which, if your car has one, is usually in the trunk. The reset mechanism is designed to turn the fuel pump off in a crash, but occasionally a bad bump or a minor rear-end collision can activate it.

On an older model, ensure that the ignition wires — the thick wires that lead to each spark plug — are firmly seated in the distributor cap. The wire in the center of the cap, which leads to the coil, should be firmly seated at both ends.

Change a Flat

For a flat tire, you can call for road service or change it yourself if your car is safe from oncoming traffic and you are in an area with no other known risks. Here's how: First, park the car on a hard, flat, level surface. Set the brake and block the wheel diagonally opposite the flat tire with wheel chocks or roadside rocks or branches.

Before lifting the car with the jack, loosen the lug nuts on the flat tire. Check your owner's manual to verify how to use the jack and where to place it. Then raise the car, finish removing the lug nuts, pull the flat tire off the hub and put on the spare. Tighten the lug nuts with your fingers, making sure the spare wheel is snug and flat against the hub. Next, lower the car to the ground and finish tightening each lug nut with a wrench. Place the jack, tools and flat tire in the trunk, remove the rocks, branches or chocks, and drive on.

Never change a tire when the car is on a hill or soft ground, and never crawl under a car supported only with a jack intended for tire changes. Also be aware that not all spares are created equal. Note any speed, load or distance limits that affect your car while the spare is in use.

Loosen Lug Nuts

If the lug nuts are so tight that you can't loosen them by hand, try lifting on one side of the T-wrench while pushing down with your foot on the other side.

Before you have to change a flat in an emergency, review the owner's manual and practice the procedure in your driveway. The manual outlines quirks that may affect your car, such as a temporary spare that will fit only on the rear. If your front tire goes flat, you'll need to put the spare on the rear, and then move the good rear tire to the front. It's best to discover such surprises before you have to change a tire by the side of the road.

Position the Tire

You can use the T-wrench to raise or lower the tire into position.

Jump-Start a Dead Battery

A good samaritan often is willing to lend a healthy battery so you can jump-start your vehicle. However, you must do the connections correctly.

If both vehicles have a negative ground — and most will, unless one is a 40-year-old English sports car — position the car with the good battery so that the jumper cables can reach the dead battery. Turn off the engine and open the hood. Identify the positive and negative terminals on both batteries. These are often labeled with "POS" or a plus sign, and "NEG" or a minus sign. The cable leading to the positive terminal often has red insulation; insulation on the wire going to the negative terminal is usually black.

SAFETY Countless motorists are injured attempting jump-starts. Batteries can explode and spray acid. You should wear protective clothing and eye protection. Never jump-start a battery that is damaged, leaking, frozen, low on electrolyte or discharging smoke or foul odors from the vents. Have the car towed instead. Don't jump-start a car with remote connection points leading to an out-of-sight battery since you can't assess the battery's condition. If your car has a maintenance-free battery, check the hydrometer in the top of the cover and follow instructions on the battery case to determine whether jump-starting is advisable. Never smoke or have an open flame near the battery, which can give off explosive hydrogen gas. Don't pound on either battery or flex the mounting posts to get a better connection. Be sure that both batteries have the same voltage.

Connect the red jumper cable clamp to the positive terminal of the dead battery. Connect the other end of the red jumper cable to the positive terminal of the live battery. Connect the black jumper cable clamp to the negative terminal of the live battery. Connect the other end of the black jumper cable to a metal part of the engine block in the car that won't start. Be sure to get a good connection. **Note:** Always connect *positive* to *positive* and *negative* to the disabled vehicle's ground, which should also be *negative*. Never use another connection point.

Jump-Start a Battery

Dead Battery   Live Battery

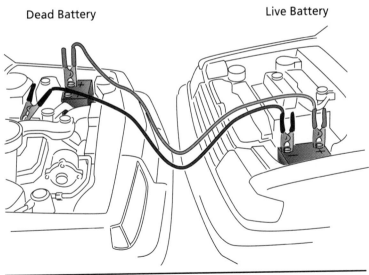

When you jump-start a dead battery, ensure you connect positive to positive and negative to a ground.

Start the disabled car, and then disconnect the cables in reverse order. If the car doesn't start right away, start the "live" car and let it idle for several minutes. Try again to start the disabled car while the other car keeps running. When the disabled car starts, remove the cables in reverse order. If the disabled car doesn't start after you've completed all the steps, don't grind away on the starter. Something else is also wrong with the vehicle.

Refuel Empty Tank

People do run out of gas. Sometimes the gauge gives a false reading. Other times, drivers simply forget to refuel. Running out of fuel is not only an annoyance, it also can cause damage. As the fuel supply is exhausted, the pump may suck dirt or sediment settled on the bottom of the tank into the fuel system, where it can clog filters and fuel lines — or worse yet, the carburetor or fuel injectors. Some vehicles with an in-tank fuel pump also need fuel to cool and lubricate the pump.

Pouring a few gallons of fuel into an empty tank won't give you an immediate restart. In a car with a mechanical fuel pump, you'll have to crank the engine for several seconds to prime the fuel lines. A fuel-injected car with an electric pump may require several cranking cycles to restore normal fuel pressure in the lines. If the car starts and runs smoothly, you're lucky. If not, you'll need professional assistance.

Add Coolant

If your radiator has a leak or the engine boils over, you'll need to replenish coolant. Never remove a pressurized radiator cap on a car with a hot engine — or even a warm one. If your car leaks coolant, you may be able to tighten a hose clamp or perform another minor repair by the side of the road, but *only after the engine has cooled* — a process that might take hours. You then can refill the radiator and drive on for service. If the engine has boiled over, coolant loss is a symptom of a bigger problem that also must be fixed.

If you doubt your ability to successfully complete any procedure, hand the car over to a professional. You'll be safer and the car will be much less likely to suffer additional damage.

Finding Right Repair Facility

When your vehicle breaks down away from home, picking a garage isn't easy. Start by looking for the AAA Approved Auto Repair certification. Even if you aren't a AAA member, you can rest assured that AAA has reviewed these garages' technician training, equipment, facilities, business practices and customer satisfaction scores.

If your newer car is still under warranty, you can have it towed to a dealer that sells your make. In rural areas where dealers for all makes aren't available, some manufacturers let a dealer that sells another one of its makes handle emergency warranty work. A Ford dealer could work on a Mercury, for instance, a Chevrolet dealer could repair a Pontiac, or a Chrysler dealer could fix a Dodge. Call the toll-free number in the owner's manual for details.

If neither option is available, size up a service facility as best you can by appearance. Generally, good service facilities look successful. While you always hear stories about people who get great service from an isolated garage that looks as if time has passed it by, you're more likely to be satisfied with a shop whose owners take pride in its appearance, have invested in the latest equipment and can fix cars quickly.

Be wary of a shop with little obvious traffic from local residents and weeds growing between dust-covered cars waiting for service. Also be concerned if the shop has an obvious shortage of modern tools and test equipment. Most successful shops today use computers.

Before authorizing repairs, call the local Better Business Bureau, Department of Consumer Affairs or AAA. If you don't like what you hear, you'd be better off having your car towed to a more reputable facility.

Some insurance policies help you with hotels and meals when you break down far from home. Review this coverage before you start a trip so you know how to take advantage of the protection if you need it.

Buying a Safer Car

In This Chapter

• • • • • • • • • • • •

- What important vehicle safety features are rarely advertised

- What safety features to look for in your next car or truck

- How to transport children

- The role telematics can play in your safety

Over the years, the concept of what constitutes a safe car has changed, as has the willingness of buyers to embrace safety. Vehicle safety is a major concern for most of today's car and truck buyers.

The problem is that drivers often don't fully understand what makes a vehicle safe. Many believe crash testing or a vehicle's weight and size determine how safe it is — and to a degree, this is correct. However, they ignore a vehicle's active safety characteristics: its ability to respond predictably and securely to a driver's use of the steering, gas and brakes in an emergency. When active safety mechanisms or a driver's skills fall short, the car's passive safety features — the ones that protect occupants in a crash — come into play. Good brakes, acceleration capabilities and steering are often much more important to your driving survival than air bags.

Do Your Research

Consumers should include safety in their research when shopping for a new car or truck. Many annual auto-buying guides, including the *AAA Auto Guide: New Cars and Trucks*, outline a vehicle's handling capabilities in both normal driving and emergency maneuvers. In the case of AAA's guide, each vehicle's handling, braking, steering and accelerating capabilities are rated on a clear one to ten scale.

Armed with this knowledge, you can check the latest crash test results to find three or four vehicles that offer you acceptable levels of active and passive safety.

Check How It Fits

With your list in hand, it's time to go shopping. Sit in each car you've highlighted and determine how well it fits you. A car that handles well and is safe in a crash is still a poor choice if you and other drivers in the family don't fit in it comfortably. Refer to the guidelines in Chapter 1, Getting Set Behind the Wheel.

Test Drive It

Test drive each vehicle that fits you well. Take it out on a bright, sunny day to check for distracting reflections. Then go back and drive it at night to check headlight performance and instrument panel lighting. Your drive should reflect the roads and conditions you normally face.

Don't be satisfied with a quick spin around the dealer's parking lot. If you need to rent a car before buying, rent the model you are considering purchasing. The more exposure to the vehicle you have before you plunk down your cash, the better.

SAFETY Instrument panel lighting has improved greatly. Back-lighted or electroluminescent displays can be extremely easy to use at night. Some panel light colors, however, may be hard on your eyes and some may be nearly invisible to people with certain forms of color blindness. Before you buy a vehicle, test drive it at night.

Look Into Passive Safety Features

A vehicle's passive safety is determined by how well it protects you in a crash. To get the most protection possible, you must buckle up and properly adjust the seat, mirrors and head restraint before every trip.

Review Crash Test Data

Crash test data will tell you some of what you need to know about your vehicle's passive safety systems. Three tests garner the majority of publicity and have become the standards for vehicle comparisons: a full-frontal-barrier crash test, an offset-barrier crash test and a side-impact crash test.

The National Highway Traffic Safety Administration, a U.S. Department of Transportation agency, grades the performance of the vehicles it tests on a scale of one to five stars in frontal and side-impact tests. In the frontal-barrier test, a vehicle going 35 mph is driven into an immovable barrier at a 90-degree angle. Test dummies in the two front seats record the forces that could cause injury or death. The side-impact test runs a sled into the driver's side of a vehicle, once to measure injuries to a dummy in the driver's seat and another time to make the same measurements on a dummy in the seat behind the driver.

The side-impact test has generated controversy for two reasons. First, the test sled is about as high as a typical passenger car, although nearly half of all vehicles now sold in this country are trucks with higher front structures. An impact from a truck would generate markedly different results. Second, head injuries to the dummy aren't measured, as they are in the frontal-barrier test. Instead, engineers measure the compression and acceleration that the ribs, spine and internal organs would suffer to determine potential thoracic injuries.

The Insurance Institute for Highway Safety performs the offset-barrier test, in which the vehicle strikes a slightly flexible object. Unlike the frontal-barrier test, which involves the vehicle's entire frontal structure, the offset-barrier test involves only 40 percent of the front

DID YOU KNOW?	More and more ads for new vehicles are including the number of stars earned in frontal-barrier and side-impact crash tests. This chart explains what the stars mean.	
	Chance of Serious Injury	
	Frontal Test	Side Test
★ ★ ★ ★ ★	Up to 10%	Up to 5%
★ ★ ★ ★	11% to 20%	6% to 10%
★ ★ ★	21% to 35%	11% to 20%
★ ★	36% to 45%	21% to 25%
★	46% or more	26% or more

structure on the driver's side. The rigorous test exceeds the forces generated in 98 percent of all offset frontal collisions.

Buyers seeking a car with good passive safety should pay attention to all three tests. The frontal-barrier crash greatly stresses the vehicle's restraint systems: the seat belts and air bags. The offset-barrier crash severely tests vehicle structure. Intrusion — when the collision's force causes the instrument panel, steering wheel or floor surfaces to invade the passenger compartment — commonly occurs in this test. The side-impact crash indicates how a vehicle performs when hit in the side, one of the most dangerous types of crashes.

Crumple Zones

A vehicle's crumple zones are areas designed to compress, or crumple, in a crash to absorb the impact's energy. In this frontal crash, all of the body deformation is confined to the frontal structure.

Modern cars and trucks use crumple zones to protect passengers in a front or rear collision. The vehicle structure that houses the engine or forms the trunk is sacrificed in a controlled manner to lessen the forces that passengers would bear in a crash. The goal is to make the vehicle's far ends easy to deform. As the damage nears the passenger compartment, as it would in a severe collision, the structure increasingly resists crumpling.

The passenger compartment shouldn't crumple. If it does, the likelihood of passenger injury or death increases substantially. Unfortunately, the passenger compartment will be violated in a severe collision, as it often is in the offset-barrier test. While all vehicles incorporate crumple zones, some do it better than others. The latest test results will guide you.

All Seat Belts Are Not Created Equal

Regardless of the type of collision — frontal, side, rear or rollover — seat belts are your first line of defense. However, not all seat belts are created equal. Some offer the added advantage of pretensioners. Others have force-limiting devices. A few provide both.

Pretensioning devices, which may be triggered by the same sensors that deploy the air bag, remove slack in the belt that might result from wearing bulky clothing, for example. They let the belt begin to restrain you immediately in a collision. The gain in safety from pretensioners is impressive.

Force limiters do just what the name implies. If the collision is so severe that the pressures exerted by the seat belt could injure your chest, the force limiter will spool out a little webbing. This lets your torso move farther forward and reduces the injury-producing forces. In modern cars, safety engineers coordinate the movement with air-bag deployment so you won't reach the bag until it has fully inflated.

For the ultimate in passive safety, buy a car with both features. If you're considering a used vehicle, look for lap and shoulder belts in every seating position, rather than lap belts alone. After a crash, have your seat belts checked and replaced if needed. The weight of your body can stretch or damage the belt so that it no longer offers full protection. The inertial reel mechanism that locks the webbing can also be damaged in a crash.

> **DID YOU KNOW?**
>
> While seat belts are crucial to getting the most from your vehicle's passive safety features, they are considered active devices since you must buckle up. Because they deploy automatically in a crash, air bags are considered passive devices. Never forget to buckle the lap belt in a vehicle with automatic shoulder belts and a manual lap belt that must be fastened separately. Using only the automatic shoulder belt will significantly compromise your safety.

Air Bags Get Smarter

Just as seat belts have become more complex, so, too, have air bags. Many can take into account seat placement, passenger position and crash dynamics before deploying with appropriate speed and force. In some cases, the air bag won't deploy if no one is seated in front of it, if the person is out of position or if the passenger is a small child. Some designs also consider whether the passenger is wearing a seat belt.

In addition to front air bags for the driver and passenger, many cars and trucks now offer side and side-curtain air bags, either standard or as an option. Side air bags can be mounted in the door panel or in the seat's side bolster. Most are designed to protect your torso in a side impact. Side-curtain air bags deploy from the roof and are designed to protect your head in a side impact. They also reduce the likelihood of ejection from the vehicle. Some vehicles slow the deflation of these bags for several seconds so they can better protect occupants during multiple rollovers. The delay should have little or no effect on your ability to get out of the vehicle after a side-impact collision that doesn't result in a rollover.

The arrival of side air bags demonstrates how important safety has become to consumers. Federal standards neither require nor regulate them. Side air bags may complicate travels with children, who often are out of position because of restlessness or because they fall asleep in an unusual position. Some manufacturers offer door-mounted

Air Bags

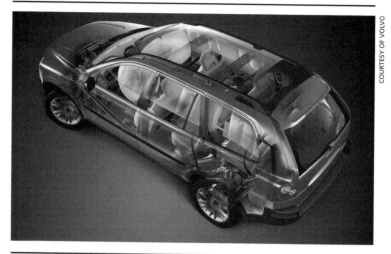

COURTESY OF VOLVO

Modern air bags are getting "smarter." Many won't deploy if no one is seated in front of them or if the person is out of position, too small or not wearing a seat belt. Deploying air bags always emit some powder so the bag unfolds without sticking.

side air bags for the rear passenger compartment, where children should ride. Parents should carefully consider the advantages and disadvantages of this feature before buying a new vehicle.

Keep Children Safe

LATCH System Boosts Safety

Difficulties installing appropriate child-safety seats properly can complicate travels with young children. Fortunately, newer vehicles feature the LATCH system, which stands for lower anchors and tethers for children. LATCH features mounting bars hidden between the lower and back cushions of the rear seats and an upper tether behind the seat.

Given that safety seats used with the vehicle's seat belts are installed improperly about 80 percent of the time, as has been observed during National Safe Kids Campaign checkup events, the new system comes none too soon. Still, parents often discover that even with a LATCH-equipped car and a compatible child seat, installation can take a surprising amount of time. Retrofit kits can make some older child-safety seats compatible with the LATCH system. If you have additional questions, visit www.aaasafejourney.org for helpful information.

Children Should Ride in Back

Infants and toddlers are safer riding in the back seat in a size-appropriate, properly installed child-safety seat. Once the child outgrows the seat, an appropriate booster seat makes sense. Never install a rear-facing infant carrier in front of an air bag. Some two-seat vehicles, which have no back seat, let you turn off the passenger side air bag, and you should do so when a young child is your passenger (in an appropriately installed safety seat). Other vehicles require you to use a special seat that deactivates the air bag automatically when it's installed in the front passenger seat.

Telematics: Safety and Security

New to the automotive field, telematics devices provide a range of communication and navigation services. Since this is a new field, the definition of telematics is still open to some discussion. As AAA defines it, telematics should enhance your safety in several ways.

Its navigation capabilities will guide you with verbal commands when you drive through unfamiliar territory so that you never need to take your eyes off the road to look at a map. This navigation function will also enhance safety when it gives you ample warning of an approaching exit and tells you whether the exit is on the right or left side of the road.

Many telematics devices use global positioning satellite technology and wireless cellular telephone communications to provide additional services. For example, in the event of a crash that deploys the air bags, the vehicle's telematics system will alert the telematics service center of the accident and show the vehicle's location. A customer service representative using a cellular connection will immediately attempt to reach the vehicle's driver. If the representative is unable to do this, or if the driver is reached and requests help, the telematics service center representative will call authorities in the area of the crash for assistance and direct help to the vehicle.

Telematics also provides a motorist's exact location to assist with police, fire, medical dispatch and roadside assistance following a vehicle breakdown. Other safety features include remote door locking and unlocking, and remote vehicle diagnostics, which includes the ability to detect a weak battery before it disables the car or truck. Telematics devices also allow authorities to track the movement of a stolen vehicle. All of these services enhance safety.

Telematics systems are now either standard or optional equipment on models from General Motors, Ford, Mercedes-Benz, BMW, Acura, Infiniti and others. Soon, telematics services may also be accessible through wireless handsets or cell phones.

Some suppliers of telematics systems want to expand the range of services to include entertainment and general information not related to driving or vehicle safety. Only passengers, not the driver, should use these additional services while the car is on the road. Drivers wishing to use these entertainment or information functions should park in a safe location to avoid being distracted.

Chapter 12

Avoiding Crime

In This Chapter

• • • • • • • • • • • •

- Why many cars are stolen and never recovered

- How to reduce your chances of being victimized while driving

- How telematics devices have changed the way car thieves work

- Why you should keep valuables out of sight even when you're in the car

Until the turn of the 21st century, crime statistics had been encouraging. For nearly a decade, the number of reported crimes in the United States had dropped steadily, resulting in the lowest crime rates in a generation.

This steady decline came to an abrupt halt in 2001, however, when the number of murders, robberies, burglaries and car thefts all rose, according to a Federal Bureau of Investigation survey of crimes reported to local police departments.

Because many criminals target motor vehicles, drivers and passengers, you risk becoming a crime victim simply by owning or using an automobile. And your level of risk appears to be on the rise.

Fortunately, you can do things to lower the likelihood of being a victim behind the wheel. You also can take additional steps to protect your car once you park it on the street, in a public parking lot or even in your own garage.

Thwart Automobile Theft

Automobile theft is perhaps the most common automotive crime. More than 1 million cars are stolen annually. In some cases, they are taken for a joy ride, abandoned and then recovered. In others, they are stolen for parts and dismantled in so-called "chop shops." Thieves also switch vehicle identification numbers and attempt to use or resell a stolen vehicle. Still other vehicles are shipped overseas.

Don't Tempt Opportunistic Thieves

No doubt you've heard suggestions for reducing the likelihood of your car being stolen. Most precautions — taking the key, locking your car and parking only in well-lighted lots — are obvious but can discourage many thieves for whom stealing a vehicle is a crime of opportunity. In other words, the thief had no intention of stealing your car until he noticed the doors unlocked and the key in the ignition. Or maybe you left valuables in plain sight or concealed them while he was watching. Don't tempt this kind of car thief.

Other thieves are more selective. Rather than steal the car with the key in the ignition and the doors unlocked, they search for a specific model, usually for its parts. Once stolen, it will be dismantled at a chop shop and its parts will be sold quickly, in most cases to a buyer who placed a specific order. Parts that can't be disposed of in a hurry will be abandoned or scrapped.

SAFETY While hiding valuables in a parked car is better than keeping them in plain sight, leaving them at home or taking them with you is often a better bet. In many cases, car thieves are not after the car but rather the expensive items you left behind. Once they break in for your property, they also may decide to take the car to simplify transporting your stolen items. Hiding items that appeal to a thief may not be good enough either. A thief might notice you moving an expensive laptop computer from the passenger compartment to the trunk. Then when you leave, all he has to do is break into the trunk.

Who buys these parts? Perhaps a dishonest body shop or garage owner who then installs the stolen components in an unsuspecting customer's vehicle. In other cases, innocent repair businesses or people looking for used parts buy them, unaware that they are stolen.

Popular Vehicles Are Often Targets

The cars and trucks most likely to attract thieves are those that topped the sales charts eight to 10 years before. When these common older models need replacement parts to keep them on the road, their owners — who probably bought the vehicles used — either are unwilling to pay for new parts or new parts aren't readily available.

This makes owners of high-sales-volume older cars and trucks the most vulnerable to car thieves. Older Honda Accords and Civics, Toyota Camrys and Corollas, Ford F-150s and Chevrolet pickup trucks often lead the National Insurance Crime Bureau's list of the most-frequently stolen vehicles. Interestingly, many of these vehicles are worth more money when sold one part at a time — a process called "parting out" — than when offered for sale on a used-car lot.

Newer cars or trucks near borders or international ports also are at heightened risk. A thief can steal the vehicle and deliver it to a closed shipping container heading overseas or drive over the border through customs, usually into Mexico. Either way, you probably won't ever see your vehicle again.

Make Thief's Work Difficult

If a skilled thief wants your car, there's nothing you can do to keep him from getting it. Your best option is to make stealing your car so time-consuming, risky and difficult that the thief will skip yours and snatch a similar vehicle whose owner took fewer precautions.

Add to a thief's difficulties by always parking in a safe, well-lighted area, taking the key, locking the doors and using the factory-installed alarm system. Never leave a key in a hidden spot under the fender or behind the bumper. You may even want to install additional locks to protect the ignition switch and trunk latch. If your car didn't come with a factory-installed alarm system, add one.

> **DID YOU KNOW?**
>
> Pick your car alarm installer carefully. The quality of installation work varies widely from shop to shop, and a poor installation of even the world's best alarm will leave you disappointed. It could also strand you. Alarm systems that either fail or were improperly installed — both of which can keep the vehicle from starting and require it to be towed — are causing an increasing number of AAA emergency road service calls. Repair can be time consuming.

Alarms are not your only weapon against car thieves. Many telematics devices can locate a stolen vehicle by sending information from the GPS system to a response center that dispatches police. In addition, some aftermarket devices — LoJack, for instance, which is available in some areas — can guide police to your stolen car.

This new technology has prompted some thieves to leave a stolen vehicle on the street for 24 hours before taking it to a chop shop. If the car is not recovered during this period, the thieves can assume it is free of electronic homing devices and won't lead police to their shop. Homing devices can help police recover your vehicle quickly — and the sooner you get your car back, the less likely it is to have serious damage.

> **DID YOU KNOW?** Call your local police department to find out whether your community has programs designed to discourage car theft. Among the more successful initiatives is a bumper sticker that invites police to stop your car if it's on the road between 1 and 5 a.m., when many thieves work. The sticker gives police probable cause for the stop and lets them verify ownership.

Protect Yourself from Carjackers

There is a downside to alarm systems and factory-installed security measures that require special keys to start the car. Because the new countermeasures can give even highly skilled thieves trouble, a new approach to stealing cars was born: carjacking.

A carjacker doesn't bother breaking through or overpowering locks and electronic countermeasures. Instead he waits for the owner to arrive with the key, then takes the key and steals the car. One variation of the crime is the thief who approaches a car on the road, pulls a weapon and forces the driver from behind the wheel. Such attacks often happen when a car is stopped in traffic or at a red light.

Authorities say you should never resist a carjacker. Give the thief your key, back away from the car and let him go. Your car can be replaced. Your life can't.

Note: While authorities advise you not to resist a criminal, there is no way anyone or anything, including this book, can outline a single proper procedure to follow if you are the victim of a crime. Whether you should resist, yell for help, flee or hand over your keys is something you'll have to decide if you're ever in this situation. Suggestions outlined in this chapter aren't the

SAFETY No parent ever wants to experience the kidnapping of a child. To avoid the risk, never leave children unattended in a vehicle, even for just a minute. In the time it takes you to run into a convenience store, a criminal can break into your vehicle and kidnap your infant or toddler. Know, too, that leaving a child unattended in a closed vehicle for longer periods can expose the child to potentially deadly temperature extremes. Also, lock your car when it's parked at home to prevent small children from crawling inside, perhaps for a nap, and being overcome by heat or cold.

only appropriate responses — and in some circumstances they may be inappropriate, even though they come from experts. Use your best judgment.

Your vehicle offers you no protection against even small-caliber handguns. A single shot easily can break glass, and in many cases, small-caliber ammunition can penetrate your vehicle's sheet metal. If an armed carjacker confronts you, give up your vehicle and get away, even if you are locked in your car.

Unarmed carjackers also can quickly get into your vehicle, even when the doors are locked. In most cars, the side and rear tempered-glass windows break easily when struck with sufficient force. The tempering process means the windows will disintegrate into hundreds of beads rather than sharp shards when broken. This characteristic gives a thief little disincentive.

Some thieves walk among vehicles stuck in traffic looking for something attractive to steal. When they see something, they break the window, grab what they want and run. For this reason, keep your valuables, including purses or briefcases, out of sight.

Some manufacturers have started producing cars with laminated side windows that are much more difficult to break. This glass may also offer a safety advantage: Occupants in a crash are less likely to be ejected from the vehicle, a benefit that experts estimate could save more than 1,000 lives a year. However, recognize that laminated windows offer no more protection from firearms than do tempered ones.

Keep Yourself from Harm

Not all crimes associated with cars and trucks target the vehicle. Some are directed at the driver and passengers. Exercise caution each time you approach your car.

Start by having your keys ready as you walk up to your car. Don't stand next to your car fumbling in your pockets or rifling through your purse for your car keys. The delay leaves you vulnerable by giving an attacker more time to approach, rob or assault you. There's an additional advantage to having your key out as you walk up to your vehicle. If you are attacked and choose to resist, you have a weapon in your hand. If your attacker seems to want only your valuables, however, police suggest that you not resist. Fighting back only increases the chance of being injured.

Be Aware of Your Surroundings

Look for suspicious people loitering around your vehicle. If you see someone, keep walking and call the police or contact a security guard. Also be careful if a van or other large vehicle is parked next to your car. An attacker could be hiding inside.

If you are returning to your vehicle late at night after work or shopping, you may be able to have a security agent accompany you. Take advantage of the service.

Visually Check Your Vehicle

If you see a problem, such as a flat tire or a puddle of coolant under the vehicle, keep walking and call for service. Many attackers flatten a tire or cut a hose and then offer to "help." Good samaritans aren't always what they seem.

Scan Passenger Compartment

Before getting in your car, look inside the passenger compartment. Some attackers break into a vehicle and hide low on the rear floor or in the cargo area of a van, hatchback or utility vehicle to await the driver's return. If you see anything suspicious in your car as you approach it, keep walking and call the police.

Stay on Guard

Even after you've started driving, stay aware of what's going on around you. Some attackers target their victims as they drive and then follow them. If you ever feel you are being followed, don't go home, to work or to an appointment. Instead, go to a police station, an area with private security guards or a well-populated area where you are more likely to be safe. If you have a cellular phone, call the police immediately.

In other cases, a potential attacker may not wait for you to arrive at your destination. Instead, he may tap your car, either while in traffic or when stopped at a light. When you get out to assess the damage and exchange license and registration information, he proceeds to rob, assault or kidnap you or steal your car.

If someone you thought was following you hits your vehicle, or if the crash circumstances or other driver make you suspicious, keep driving until you reach a safe area. Get a description of the other vehicle, including its license plate number and its driver and passengers. If you have a cellular phone, call the police and report the incident. Signal the other driver to follow you to a safe place until the police arrive. While the law requires you to stop after an accident, be extremely cautious about where you stop if you suspect you are in danger. Choose a location with police protection.

Be Wary of Insurance Schemes

Also be on the lookout for criminals who specialize in insurance fraud. They usually victimize teenage or older drivers, but everyone who gets behind the wheel is a potential target.

The scam starts when another driver forces you into a minor crash that seems to be your fault. This driver may even work with "witnesses" who will stop and verify that you are to blame. Since the damage is minor, the "victim" will waive a police investigation to spare you a ticket. He even may suggest exchanging identification and working the matter out without involving your insurance company so as to not risk raising your rates.

You agree, relieved to be getting off so lightly. Then, a few days, weeks or even months later, you are served with a large lawsuit for injuries the "victim" claims resulted from the crash. The fraud may even involve additional people who weren't there but will claim to have been passengers. With no police investigation, no photographs and no independent witnesses, it's your word against theirs. Good luck.

For more suggestions, review Chapter 5, Handling and Avoiding Accidents.

Just a few simple precautions can lower your likelihood of becoming crime's latest victim. Be alert and stay aware of the potential for danger. A little extra caution can significantly enhance your safety.

Chapter 13

Driving Overseas

In This Chapter

• • • • • • • • • • • •

- What document you should have in addition to your license

- How much insurance you need

- What to look for in a rental car

- How to drive on the left side of the road

For more and more travelers, a vacation means going overseas. No matter which nation you visit, you'll find plenty to do and see. However, as you plan your trip, you may discover that going where you want, when you want, will be easier if you rent a car. Should you do it?

Many popular destinations offer excellent public transportation. You'll often find it easier, more enjoyable, less expensive and more restful to use trains, buses, taxis and even short flights to get where you want to go. In some cases, you may not have a choice: A few destinations forbid foreign visitors from driving. You might consider hiring a car with a professional driver in some countries.

Nonetheless, many travelers prefer having a car. For large families or groups, having a vehicle can even make the vacation less expensive, despite high fuel prices in many countries.

Plan Ahead for Overseas Driving

If renting a car on your next overseas vacation appeals to you, there are things you should consider.

Study Each Country's Laws

Each country has its own driving rules and regulations. It's up to you to know and understand them before taking to the road. Start by contacting the consulates of countries you plan to visit. Many can give you the information you need. In addition, the U.S. Department of State has amassed information about driving in other countries. To access it, go to its website: travel.state.gov/road_safety.html.

Consider an International Driving Permit

Although not required in all countries, many travelers have found an International Driving Permit to be invaluable. The State Department authorizes AAA to sell these permits to holders of U.S. driver's licenses before they leave the country. An IDP provides important driver information in many languages, including English. The passport-sized document is a translation of the license you carry and tells officials overseas that it is valid and should be honored. You must have your state-issued driver's license in your possession to make your International Driving Permit valid.

Carry Adequate Insurance

Before driving in a foreign country, make sure you have adequate insurance. Your auto insurance policy likely doesn't cover driving outside the United States, Canada

DID YOU KNOW?

The International Driving Permit is written in many languages: Arabic, Chinese, English, French, German, Italian, Japanese, Portuguese, Russian, Spanish and Swedish. It can save you time when you rent a car, cross a border, are stopped by police or have a crash. It can be particularly handy if you don't speak the language of the country you are visiting.

or Mexico. Many policies won't cover you in Mexico or Canada either. Before you drive beyond U.S. borders, review your insurance policy carefully.

If your policy covers you in the country you plan to visit, make sure it meets that country's required liability limits. For example, Canada specifies $200,000 in liability coverage — an amount not all states require. If you need extra coverage, determine whether you should make the arrangements before you leave or when you arrive at your destination.

Most rental car agencies can arrange insurance for you. Generally, opt for no less protection than you have with your auto policy in the United States. In addition to reviewing your auto coverage, verify that your health insurance covers you while traveling abroad as well.

Know What to Expect in a Rental Car

Tourists who rent a car overseas may be in for a surprise. Many vehicles in foreign rental fleets come with a manual transmission, although you may be able to upgrade to an automatic for an extra charge. In addition, many vehicles are small. They may hold a typical family of four but won't have room for luggage. Check ahead of time if these issues are important to you.

In addition, some accessories that we take for granted in American rental cars — air conditioning, for instance — may not be available or may entail a costly upgrade.

Regardless of how your rental car is equipped, make sure it has no signs or stickers that would single it out as a rental car. Criminals often prey on tourists. Your appearance and language likely will make you stand out as the tourist you are. Don't provide additional confirmation of your tourist status while you are on the road.

Review the condition of your rental car carefully before you leave with the vehicle. Many foreign companies are far more particular about minor dings and scratches than are domestic companies. Make sure any cosmetic problems are noted clearly on the contract. In addition, check for all accessories that can be easily removed from the vehicle, such as the spare tire and jack. Some countries also require that every car be equipped with a first aid kit, fire extinguisher and a warning triangle. If you're driving in a country that requires these items, make sure your rental car has them before you leave.

If you plan to pick up a vehicle in one city and leave it in another, ask about drop-off charges or one-way service fees. Fees vary by location and in some cases can be substantial. Also, find out whether the rental agency charges a fee if you return the car before the time your contract specifies.

If your contract requires you to return the vehicle with a full fuel tank, check the calendar to make sure that your return date doesn't fall on a day when the gas station may not be open, usually a Sunday or holiday. Failing to fill the tank could be expensive.

Do as Natives Do

If you're traveling with children, check to see whether the countries you're visiting have age requirements for front-seat passengers. Also, most countries require the use of seat belts for passengers in all seating positions. There also may be specific requirements for the use of infant, child or booster seats.

Before renting a car abroad, obtain road maps of the areas where you plan to drive and plot your route in advance. While traveling between towns and in smaller cities may be easy, many major cities have heavy traffic, narrow streets, strict regulations governing the use of private cars and confusing traffic patterns. Get as much information as possible before leaving home. Also avoid driving at night.

In major cities, many tourists find it easier to return the car to the rental agency and then rely on mass transit. Parking is difficult in many cities, and thieves often target cars. Leave nothing visible in the passenger compartment when you park, and if possible, don't leave anything locked in the trunk either.

Adapt to Regional Driving Styles

Perhaps most difficult for tourists traveling overseas is the need to cope with strange signs and driving styles. Just as driving styles and traffic patterns differ among American cities, they differ from region to region overseas. In some areas, motorists are polite. In others, they are aggressive. For an enjoyable vacation, you'll need to cope with either style.

DID YOU KNOW? When overseas, think metric. Distances are measured in kilometers, not miles, and speeds are posted in kilometers per hour, not miles per hour, except in Great Britain. You buy gasoline in liters, and it takes 3.785 of them to equal one gallon. Metric fuel-economy computers display how many liters of fuel it takes to go 100 kilometers, so the more slowly you drive, the lower the display number will be. For speed or distance conversions, multiply kilometers by 0.62 to find the distance or speed in miles. Similarly, miles divided by 0.62 equals distance or speed in kilometers.

Conversion Chart

KPH	MPH
30	18
50	31
80	50
90	56
100	62
110	68
120	74
130	80

Heed Others' Need for Speed

Many Americans come home from their overseas vacation marveling at how fast traffic flows in many foreign countries. In some areas, speed limits either don't exist or are poorly enforced. As a result, motorists often travel well above the posted limit. While you may be tempted to join them in the high-speed lane, you'd be much better off obeying the speed limit. When speed limits are enforced in many countries, police can be exceptionally thorough, and steep fines must be paid on the spot. In addition, many countries rely on photographic enforcement. You could be caught speeding and not know it until your rental car agency forwards notice of your fine.

In recent years, discipline on American multilane highways has eroded. Slow drivers clutter the left lane while fast drivers pass on the right. In many countries, particularly in Europe, lane discipline is strictly observed. It is illegal to pass on the right, and motorists simply don't do it. By the same token, they don't have to. Drivers who are passing slower vehicles leave the left lane willingly to let faster traffic pass.

On European roads without speed limits, drivers sometimes travel in excess of 150 mph — 240 kph — in the left lane. When passing a slower vehicle, even at speeds greater than 80 mph, carefully watch your rearview mirror for high-speed travelers. Although they're a considerable distance behind you, they often flash their lights to say they'd like you out of their way by the time they catch up to you. You should gladly oblige them.

Narrow Roads

In town, narrow streets may intimidate you. Keep in mind that older cities were laid out well before the automobile was invented. Local drivers pass much closer to your car than you might find comfortable. Space margins are so tight that many Europeans who park on the street fold in their vehicle's outside mirrors to avoid damage from passing vehicles. In some Latin American countries, drivers leave their cars in neutral so car attendants can push vehicles bumper-to-bumper to conserve space. If being this close to other vehicles makes you uncomfortable, think carefully before renting a car.

Learn Road Signs

You'll also have to memorize new road signs. Generally, circular signs serve a regulatory function and tell you what you can and can't do. Triangular signs warn of a problem ahead, while rectangular signs provide information. Fortunately, many signs use symbols rather than words to convey their message.

Danger Signs

Intersection with a road the users of which must give way

Ten percent grade — dangerous descent and steep ascent

Carriageway narrows   Two-way traffic   Roundabout

Uneven road   Ridge   Dip

Slippery road   Loose gravel   Falling rocks

Danger Signs

Pedestrian
crossing

Children

Cyclists entering
or crossing

Road works

Cattle or other animals crossing

Airfield

Intersection where the priority is that
prescribed by the general priority rule
in force in the country

Light signals

Right bend
(left bend if
symbol is
reversed)

Double bend,
the first to
the left (first
bend to right
if symbol is
reversed)

Dangerous
bend

Other dangers

Danger Signs

Cross-wind

Swing bridge

Road leads onto
a quay or
river bank

Level-crossing
with gates or
staggered
half-gates

Other level
crossings

Intersection with
a tramway line

Priority Signs

Advance
warning of
"give way"

Give way

Stop
(new)

Stop
(old)

Priority road
(yellow center)

End of
priority

Oncoming
traffic has
priority

Priority over
oncoming
traffic

Signs placed in the immediate vicinity of level-crossings

Regulatory Signs

No entry   Closed to all vehicles in both directions   Overtaking prohibited

No left turn (no right turn if the symbol is reversed)

Maximum speed limit   End of speed limit (bar may be gray or red)

Think Backward

Perhaps most challenging is motoring in a country where the people drive on the left side of the road. Nothing compares to getting off an airplane after a 10-hour flight and immediately hopping into a rental car and driving on what — for you, at least — is the wrong side of the street. Get a good night's sleep before attempting to drive on the left.

> **DID YOU KNOW?**
>
> Driving on the left side of the road is common in countries worldwide. In Europe, motorists in the Channel Islands, Cyprus, Ireland, Malta and the United Kingdom all drive on the left. In Asia, the list includes Hong Kong, India, Indonesia, Japan, Malaysia, Nepal, Pakistan, Singapore and Thailand. Botswana, Mozambique, South Africa, Kenya, Tanzania and Uganda are among African nations where driving on the right is definitely wrong. Australia and New Zealand also drive on the left, as do destinations in the Caribbean, such as Barbados and Jamaica, and South America, including Guyana and Suriname.

A little mental practice in advance can make the transition easier. As you drive at home, think about how you'll have to drive at your destination. Imagine driving on the left side of the road, keeping to the left as you take corners and going clockwise around traffic circles.

Remember the phrase, "Keep left, look right." "Keep left" recognizes that you must drive on the left side of secondary roads. On limited-access highways, often called dual carriageways in Great Britain, the slow lane is the left lane, and you will "keep left" except to pass. "Look right" indicates the direction from which cross traffic reaches your car first at intersections. This advice also is critical for pedestrian safety. When crossing a street, look to the right first, not the left.

Think your way through intersections and corners before you arrive at the turn. For people not used to driving on the left, corners can be a particular challenge. Remember to "keep left" and refrain from either drifting too wide or cutting the corner too tightly.

Navigate a Rotary

"Keep left, look right" should continue to be your mantra in a rotary. Yield to vehicles already in the rotary as you enter, and drive in a clockwise direction.

When in doubt, follow the locals. Years of experience have honed their driving, so you probably can count on them to handle intersections and other potentially difficult traffic patterns correctly.

Go clockwise at rotaries or roundabouts. As in most areas of the United States, unless directed otherwise, you will yield to traffic already in the rotary as you enter from the left side of the street.

Don't panic at the sight of parked cars facing the wrong way. Drivers overseas often park on opposite sides of the street. If you round a corner and see nothing but the headlights of parked cars on the left and tail lights of other parked vehicles on the right, don't become unnerved and go back to driving on the right. You still have to "keep left, look right."

Watch the left side of your vehicle. Don't assume that your ability to sense where the right side of your car is when driving at home means you can automatically judge the position of the left side when driving from the opposite seat. Curbs and poles may be closer than you think.

Before you return to the United States, start thinking, "keep right, look left." As hard as it is to believe, you'll need to readjust even after only a week of driving on the other side of the road.

At least you won't have to adjust to changes in basic vehicle controls when you rent a car with a right-side driver's seat. The gas, brake and clutch pedals are in the same position relative to the seat. In addition, the directional signal stalk is on the left side of the steering column and wiper controls are on a stalk on the right, just the way many imports in this country do it. In Asia, however, or if you rent a Japanese car in Great Britain, you'll likely find the directional signal and wiper stalks reversed.

Drive long enough in some countries and eventually you'll come across a multiple roundabout. Such dual rotaries, one right after another, usually are at complex intersections. They can be intimidating at first sight, but take them one at a time and follow the normal rules for navigating a rotary.

If, after considering the added demands of driving overseas, you decide not to try it, you have lots of company. Many foreign visitors to the United States make the same decision for the same reasons. Whatever you decide, enjoy your trip and travel safely.

Chapter 14

In Conclusion

In This Chapter

• • • • • • • • • • • •

- Why a clean record doesn't necessarily mean you're a good driver

- Why it's important to keep up with driving and safety advances

- How fatigue and distractions can be deadly

- How practicing maneuvers can save you in an emergency

Driving, like life, will never be free of risk. There's plenty you can do, however, to reduce the level of risk you face behind the wheel. Many people, unfortunately, don't consider reducing risk important. Some mistakenly believe that driving is safer than it actually is. Others may have an immediate need — running late for an appointment, for instance — that outweighs thoughts of safety. Some enjoy the thrill of "pushing the envelope," as a participant in one of my classes for people who accumulate too many traffic tickets put it. And then there are the anti-social few who willingly use their cars as they would use fists in a brawl.

Yet my observations from performing countless behind-the-wheel evaluations lead me to conclude that the vast majority of motorists fall short for relatively simple reasons.

Motorists Think They Drive Well

Most people believe they are better drivers than they actually are. Many don't know what good driving is or believe they already practice it.

Take, for example, a man who was born and raised in Manhattan and never drove until, at age 40, his employer transferred him to another city. After his company's clients complained that his driving terrorized them, I evaluated his technique, at his request, and found numerous problems. Frustrated at hearing my many suggestions, he asked, "How can I be so wrong when I've never had an accident?" Obviously, luck had been with him for the three years he had been driving.

His frustration points to an obvious fact: Many people believe a crash- and ticket-free record validates their driving skill. Nothing could be further from the truth. Many people with excellent driving records crash — and die.

Even people with blemished records can refuse to accept that their driving falls short of perfection. A few years ago, I sat in on a series of interviews a local television station did with people forced to attend a class for traffic-law violators. Before the class, I watched their arrivals. More than half were five minutes late and probably left home expecting to make up time along the way.

In one case, a late arrival spied an empty parking space near the building's front door. She sped through the parking lot, ignored a stop sign posted at a blind intersection just before the space and charged into the spot, bouncing off the curb. When the reporter asked her why she had to attend the class, she replied, "I don't know. I'm a really good driver." She clearly believed what she said despite having received at least three tickets during a two-year period for significant infractions of state traffic laws.

Drivers Follow Outmoded Concepts

Although the times, vehicles, roads, traffic patterns and laws change, the concepts and ideas that many motorists learn as soon-to-be-licensed teenagers remain valid in their minds. Many continue to believe that a space cushion of "one car length for every 10 mph" will protect them, even though they really need to leave a three-second gap between their car and the vehicle in front, which at 60 mph is nearly three times the space they think they need.

Drivers also hold and turn the steering wheel incorrectly, misuse antilock brakes, fail to use new lighting systems properly, misadjust seat belts and head restraints and forget finer points of the rules and regulations that govern driving in their state.

New technology, new laws and new research one day will invalidate some of the suggestions in this book. You must make an ongoing effort to keep up with the latest advancements in driving and safety.

Drivers Don't Look Far Enough Ahead

It's too easy to fix your gaze on an area not nearly far enough ahead. Drivers in the habit of using their eyes properly reduce the risks associated with driving. By combining proper scanning habits with an adequate space margin, you significantly lower your chances of being involved in a crash. So far, no one has ever told me that he or she crashed because of having too much time or too much space to react.

Distractions Plague Motorists

Because driving doesn't always require full attention, many drivers let themselves be distracted or become inattentive. Although this usually doesn't result in a crash, you never know when it will.

Don't lose track of the traffic around you. After a few thousand miles of crash-free inattentive or distracted driving, many drivers start believing they can give driving less than their full attention all the time. Statistics show they can't.

People Drive When Tired

People who would never drive drunk willingly drive when tired. Fatigue dulls your reflexes, lessens your awareness of what's going on around you and ultimately can cause you to fall asleep. Despite this, even professional drivers believe they can battle their sleep cycles and win every time. They can't.

Motorists Aren't Prepared for Emergencies

Drivers often refuse to practice or review in their minds what they should do in an emergency. No athlete or musician can excel in a difficult situation without practice. Yet many drivers don't know what they would do if their car were to skid, if a tire were to fail or if the brakes were to give out. In an emergency, you don't have time to develop and implement an effective strategy. You should have a plan already in place.

Although driving has never been safer in the United States, there is ample room for improvement. For the most part, automobile manufacturers and highway engineers are doing their part. As a driver, you're wise to join in the effort.

Appendix

Appendix

Websites

The Internet is a great place to get information or to shop for just about anything. Here's a list — by no means complete — of some automotive websites you might find useful. AAA cannot guarantee these sites, nor does AAA necessarily agree with their content.

aaa.com — Direct access to AAA and all of its services, including the club and offices near you. The car-buying section has a new-vehicle buying tool, used-car prices and access to VIN history reports. There's also information on vehicle insurance, financing and maintenance.

aaafoundation.org — This site for AAA Foundation for Traffic Safety gives you up-to-date information on many safety issues. You'll also find real-time road weather conditions, weather radar and forecasts here.

autonews.com — The site for *Automotive News*, a major industry publication. This is where you can read up on what's happening from the manufacturers' and dealers' perspectives.

autopedia.com — A great source of information, from technical material to where to buy your next car online. It includes several bulletin boards to post your questions.

autoshop-online.com — Expert repair advice, tech tips and an introductory automotive course.

car-stuff.com — A list of links to automotive sites, from buying guides to museums.

hwysafety.org — Access the offset-barrier crash test results performed by the Insurance Institute for Highway Safety, as well as other information.

napaonline.com — Online auto parts store. AAA members receive a discount when this site is accessed through aaa.com and a purchase is made.

nhtsa.gov — Lists the latest results from frontal and side crash testing and rollover information from the National Highway Traffic Safety Administration. Also gives access to all safety-related recalls by year, make and model as well as service bulletins, reviews and complaints.

seniordrivers.org — AAA Foundation for Traffic Safety's site on senior drivers and driving safety.

Index

Index

Over 200 Ways to Travel With Someone You Trust®

AAA published its first TourBook in 1914. Today, we publish over 200 great titles including a full line of specialty travel guides. These books provide information ranging from how to compile a scrapbook to details about your favorite sports teams. Books include *Travel Tips You Can Trust, The Ultimate Fan's Guide to Pro Sports Travel, The Great National Parks, Traveling with your Grandkids, North America The Beautiful*, and many more.

Purchase AAA travel publications at participating AAA club offices, on participating club Web sites at www.aaa.com, and in fine book stores.